ÓYEME

ÓYEME

Jessica Diaz

ALEGRIA
PUBLISHING

Library of Congress Control Number: 2024901740

ISBN: 9798988174660

Published by Alegria Publishing

Book cover and layout by Carlos Mendoza

Photography and Art Direction by Jessica Diaz

To Mom & Dad, Iris & Luis

Thank you will never be enough.
I promise that I am still listening.

Please continue to guide this journey,
from your heavenly state & from within my heart.

Love Always

CONTENTS

FOREWORD

Oh, I love Jessica Diaz and oh, I love *ÓYEME* and the way it shows off, strides and stunts on the page. A radiant, swaggering, stunning journey of honoring and paying deep homage to her Bronx and Borinquen roots, this collection is full of soil, sweat, the boisterous bloom of history, of reminding us all to examine where we come from, how we show up in the world and especially who we are when we do. Each poem a revelation, a calling, a shout out, a wheeling rumble. These poems are bilingual, confident, rambunctious, bold. They do not care who is watching them. They bask in it, expect it, are hungry for it. Jessica Diaz writes the kind of poems that are unafraid and suddenly, everyone has eyes on them. These poems show off her gift, her swagger, her sheer luminosity. That is what Jessica Diaz does every time her pen hits the page. She is the sun, shining and brilliant and everlasting. She is heat lightning, fire, she is warmth and glow. She electrifies everything she touches. Her voice so singular, yet so inclusive *at the same time*. Watch the way she invites everyone in from the poem: *Taste of Native Tongues (inspired by Bronx y Nuyorican Flavas)*.

> *That's my Hood's Gumbo stewing, brewing*
> *Hecho en los calderos de nuestras abuelas y bisabuelas*
> *Bubblin' up la salsa, soul, hip hop y cumbias*
> *That rumble through sound systems, and veins*
> *Every Saturday morning cuando la gente se ponen a mover*
> *las caderas, y sus escobas*
> *Ese asopao calentandose, waiting patiently to be devoured by its Natives*
> *Bellies attentive, vibin' with the aroma*
> *Cuz we ain't neva been scared to seek out what's rightfully meant for us to eat*

This Nuyorican collection is one of birth, womanhood, sisterhood, legacy. How will these poems teach us? How will they guide us through literary traditions, images and word play that leave us hustling to hold onto the tender, the vulnerable, the tough ways in which Jessica Diaz loves and shows us how to love too. Each stanza meant to nurture, savor, season. Each line bursting with energy, baptism, invitation to take a seat and stay a long while. These poems are permanent. Lasting. Take us on the journey too. Don't let up. Heal, hold, blaze, imprint.

I have known, worked with, been inspired and moved by, learned from and been ultimately guided by Jessica Diaz for nearly twenty years. Again and again, I stand in awe of her deep love and connection to creating, cultivating and being an artist while simultaneously teaching, educating and most of all community building. That longevity, commitment, stay "with-it-ness" as she calls it, is profound and unending. Relentless. Unflinching. Unmovable. Unbreakable. Everyone at DreamYard, the nonprofit arts in education, social justice-based organization where we met, could see that every single time we were in her class. I cannot count the times I have heard, "Oh, I love Jessica Diaz," over the years. Because we do. All of us. Everyone who has ever been in her gleaming orbit. Students, co-teachers, partner educators, administrators, families, artists. We all see her. Have been seen and heard by her. Yes, yes she can hold both worlds, make us all feel valued, understood, elevated. I have seen her prepare elementary students to take the stage at poetry slams and open mic events, building confidence, inspiring ways to say yes, to get in front of the audience and shine while all the time working on her own craft and figuring out all the ways to shine alongside them. This is the true work of an artist, activist, community organizer and longtime social justice-oriented educator. This is her life's work.

ÓYEME arrives right on time. This is essential reading for anyone who is searching for themselves, trying to figure out how to exist, stand out and especially how to love themselves wholly, unafraid, confident, proud. I keep holding onto these lines that start the poem: I Am/ We Are

Let me tell you who I be -

Daughter of La Isla Borinqueña,
of Enchantment,
And cityscapes & concrete
Birthed from my Rainbow
Caressed with sponges and brillo
To soften me and toughen me up at the same time
Nurtured in the good and the bad
Strange

ÓYEME is a collection that I will teach and share with the young people I work with. It is one that I will keep close on my bookshelf to refer to and learn from, be guided by. It is one I will savor and return to again and again. "Vision is a birthright," Jessica Diaz writes, and we all believe her, because we have seen the way her vision has grown and been nurtured. The way it continues to blossom, to flourish. What luck to ride alongside Jessica Diaz in this creative and poetic world.

Ellen Hagan
Writer. Performer. Educator.
Author of: All That Shines & Blooming Fiascoes

PREFACE

We write to taste life twice, in the moment and in retrospect.
- Anaïs Nin
You must stay drunk on writing so reality cannot destroy you.
- Ray Bradbury
Tears are words that need to be written.
- Paulo Coelho

ÓYEME was birthed in quite a peculiar time, but exactly the right time. I had always toyed with the idea of writing a book, though I was never fully committed to a theme or genre. Nor had I pinpointed a specific time or place in which I would dedicate my focus to it. Then, the pandemic hit and, as they say, *"the rest is history"*.

I've always identified myself as a creative, an artist; but struggled to give it equal footing in my life to grow - being that I am also a long-time educator. I had journal entries, and prompts and poems collected across several notebooks as far back as 2007. But, again, never set a target as to when I would actually focus on sifting through all of this and make sense of it. It was when I was forced to be still and reflect on those things that I feel passion for, empowered by and comfort in that I was reintroduced to the page.

I hadn't picked up my pen to consistently write poetry in a very long time prior to the pandemic. I had some one-offs. Spurts of inspiration, motivation. But nothing consistent. My immersion into the new world of online open mics and virtual writing workshops is what reignited the spark and, honestly, kept me sane. It was such a scary time of isolation and uncertainty, that connecting within creative spaces online served as therapy. Helping to make sense of what was happening in the moment as well as encouraging me to reflect on and dissect all those things that had gotten me to this present. In this introspection and within these virtual communities is where I stumbled into the opportunity to vye for a scholarship through **ALEGRIA** publishing to craft my first book. It was one of those opportunities I didn't realize how much I needed until I got it. And, there it was. A new journey being documented into my history.

ÓYEME is a collection of introspection, reflection on relationships, love and life lessons and how these show up within the context of our culture. Questions that prompted some of these pieces as well as ones that surfaced during the writing process were:
What is valued in life? What isn't?
How do we show up in our communities? Where can we foster positive impact?
How do we connect to our true selves and to others we care for?
What are those constants about ourselves that remain when all the hurt and insecurities endured are stripped away?
What are we searching for, and how do we know when we've found it?
How can we hold onto internal peace for ourselves?
What does happiness look like and feel like for me?

I've been asked before: *Why do you write?* The answer is simple - because I can. As short a reply as that can come off as cocky. But, it isn't. Rather, it's an act of defiance and a proclamation of significance. My purpose is to prove it's possible - to be multifaceted when society tries to peg us and put us into a predetermined box. I have set my sights on being a writer because I need to have the audacity to say that I can. As a Bronx-native and woman of Puerto Rican descent, I have had my fair share of challenges in navigating educational and professional spaces that took one look at me and just assumed I was not good enough. Assumed that I didn't have the smarts or work ethic or "with-it-ness" to achieve goals I'd set. *How dare someone like me be so ambitious and set such lofty goals for myself?*

It is still an unfortunate reality that BIPOC voices, especially those of women, are seldom highlighted and celebrated. Our cultures, our stories and our perspectives are valid and worthy of being shared. That is the driving force behind this book. Hence the title, *ÓYEME* - which translates to *listen to me*, as in one's internal voice as well as the guidance of those voices of our trusted loved ones, griots and spirit guides.

After all this time navigating life and its societal roadblocks, I've finally come to a space where I honestly don't care what anyone's perceived notions of what I should or shouldn't do are. If I'd focused on all the things people told me I shouldn't waste my time on because I'd never be able to access them, I'd be living inside a cage of flesh - just existing in space but too afraid to impact it. I've accepted and am fully in love with my duality now. I can embrace all the sides of myself and celebrate them loudly, unapologetically. I can be The Artist & The Academic. The Poetic Philosopher - with the cool facade hugging an electric core. Growing in all ways, always. Speaking out loud, and talking with my hands so you can really feel my point. The Centered Diagonal. Yeah, that's me.

So as you begin your reading journey through *ÓYEME*, I hope you share smiles and shed tears with me. Connect to warm memories and dissect the not so pleasant ones. Think fondly about where you've been, and get filled with excitement with all the possibilities as to where you'll go next. The answers are always within reach. We just need to *listen*.

CHAPTER 1

An Introduction

Yes -
I am that Puerto Rican girl from The Bronx
Old enough to know betta
But, brazen enough to do it anyways
Oozing youthfulness & whimsy & persistence
Nuyooo-Riii-I-CAN
Bathed by the waves of Mi Isla
Safeguarded by the callous covering my Latina skin
Born & Bred in a burning borough
Discarded oftentimes before the 1st match was ever even lit

I ask: *Do I deserve this?*
Am I the exception when I should be the Universal Rule?

"The Story Begins..."

Entering this cold world through an alternate escape route
January 20th
Leaving the comfort of womb
Christened with the Holy Trinity -
Salud
Dinero
Y Amor
Arms opened wide and into the waiting brazos of Nueva York

Begins with "I"

I Am Here.
In this space and on this planet to serve –
Be it a plate, some face or some gems
I Am Here.
You will notice. You will hear me. You don't have a say in the matter.
Not. This. Time.

My servitude takes many forms. And I be the one to determine how that takes shape. It's taken quite some time for me to realize that it has always been my choice to make. But, I see it now. I feel it now. I won't let this slip out of my realm of reality again.

I've said for a very long time that I wanted a life filled with passion & purpose. What exactly that meant and how that "purpose & passion" would show themselves, I don't think I ever really got that far into my thinking... But, the last 4 years have put a lot of things in perspective to help me figure out what this "passion & purpose" are supposed to be – at least for me.

First, I have to love Me with abandon. I have to. There's no way around it. I need to love up on me as much as I have loved, and continue to pour love into others and things that I believe to be important. I need to feel about myself the way that I feel when I taste that first creamy dream of a bite into the best cheesecake ever and my eyes roll around crazy and I start going Ohhh my Gawdddd, savoring it soooo damn slow that I SWEAR I can savor its flavor foreva... as much as I love hearing my "framily" (Yes, friends who are family) cackle and say, "Yooooooo!" when we reminisce or listen to a crazy beat or we see some crazy ass meme that reminds us of the days when we were all rookie elementary school teachers getting broken in HARDT. I will love myself fully the way I glance at my pug, Chauncey, when he's just laying there – anywhere in our 2-bedroom apartment – being sweet, and loyal, and doting, and chill as fuck, doing his "Pug Life" thang – snoring, passing gas and making baby gurgles while he's dreaming about milkbones or

chicken wings or running in the grass or whatever he dreams about.
I need to gaze upon myself with that unrequited love and admiration
in all of my quirks, my nuances, my perfect imperfections, my
"spunk". What makes me Me. If I'm going to have passion in what I
do – anything that I do – I need to be crazy in love with myself. That
passion for my uniqueness and nurturing is what's going to translate
into whatever I lay my hands on.

Secondly, I need to trust myself beyond a shadow of a doubt. Trust
my gut. Trust my instincts. Trust that "yo no se que," whatever you
wanna call it. The whisper. The ripple. The visions & symbols of
dreams. The subtle "signs" that I swear are my parents' otherworldly
way of communicating with me from Heaven. From The AfterLife.
Another platform for life. From a vortex. From the outer corners of
outer space. Shit. It could be from Hell for all I know. Luis & Iris
Diaz were feisty when they wanted to be. They would've told you
that themselves. Straight up. "No tenían pelos en la lengua" as my
moms would say often, lol. So, IF they are in THAT place, I know
they are telling the dirtiest jokes, throwing back hella shots and Cuba
Libres and DEFINITELY dancing to some old school salsa. I say
that to say this: WHATEVER the path I choose, the journey I take
and wherever the fuck I end up, I need to trust it because I NEED to
trust that I am thoroughly equipped to maneuver that road. Twists,
turns, ups, downs, peaks, valleys – All of it. The Divine is in Me.
The Universe is in Me. Not metaphorically. But, literally. In. Me.
I'm not prescribed or subscribed into any specific religion. But, I
know that I am connected to a heartbeat within Mother Earth and
our galaxy. I know that I think the way I do, I feel the way I do and
I write the way I do because it is organic, ingrained in my spirit and
my genetics. I'm born of a people, of a culture, of a borough that
has never had a choice to NOT do it. "Ain't nuttin' to it but to do it,"
right? And I ain't dumb enough to stray from those strong family
roots.

And, lastly, I have to live Life to please Me. I AM my first line of
defense. I AM my "ryde or die". I have proven that to myself time &
time again. Not to say that I don't have a tribe who loves me because

I do, and I am so blessed to have them. But, at the end of it all, when I reach my eternal sleep number, I need to be able to look at it all and genuinely smile, be internally happy with the journey I've made, the paths I've traversed and the new ones that I paved for the next crew comin' up behind me. So I will serve – continuously with consistency. Serve kindness to my kids. Yes, all my surrogate Bronx babies. Each and every student who I have been lucky to call mine. To the kid I hope to have – in whichever form The Divine bestows it upon me. Serve sustenance in abundance in the form of hugs to my peeples – the ones where I grip you tight and force you to sway back & forth with me. In the form of long talks and sharing my do's and don'ts and maybes and not so sures. In the form of patience and quiet – giving you my ears to listen with both my brain & my heart. Giving you direct eye-contact, letting you know that I see you. Giving you the feels of how you always take my breath away in the form of these words – writing poems, and stories, and memories of U, of Me, of Us, of We so that we all can reclaim our time, our space and our brilliance TOGETHER.

I Am HERE. I AM A WRITER.

In this space and on this page to serve –
Be it a poem, some fiction or some historical gems
I Am HERE.
You will notice. You will hear me. You don't have a say in the matter.
Not. This. Time.

Inner Voice

I am as cool as a cucumber
This don't phase me
I'm too good for him, for them
They intimidated.
...well, maybe I intimidate me?

I DON'T BELIEVE YOU

I'm so iffy sometimes
Not knowin' what I want
Or is it that I'm afraid to have it?

I DON'T BELIEVE YOU

I can have it...
Yes
No reason not
Others have gotten to the top
With greater challenges to bear
Why couldn't I take it there?

I DON'T BELIEVE YOU

Challenge me to the vulnerability
Share the story that is uniquely mine
Shared with the We
Others who share similar mind
Unique is this trajectory
Rooted in history and faith
I will be the one to set this course straight

I DON'T BELIEVE YOU

Shutdown the internal noise
Radio silence the static
Get into the curves, the grooves, the squiggles
Letters stripped bare on these pages
To seduce and entice
I can't flatline in the end
With greatness is the only way this can manifest

I DON'T BELIEVE YOU

Oye, Nena...
(Aviso Número Uno De Mama)

Sola la hago y sola la pago
Así nadie me puede decir que le debo algo
Este cuerpo es mío
Para ser lo que me da la gana
Y a quien me da la gana
Cuando me da las ganas
Porque la gente puede tener sus opiniones
Pero, al fin, quien sabe lo que necesito
Soy Yo

Be PEN

I Use my Pen for Good,
Not Evil.

To Flow
To Create
To Explore
To Navigate
Words CAN circumvent the globe

Just as the "mighty sword,"
I slay demons
Kill stereotypes and
Abolish All Doubt

I create doctrine – Earthly & Spiritual, Even Holy
Bring voice to the inaudible,
and leave speechless the naysayers

Permanent & Poignant
Sharp, and to the point.

I am quite the crafty warrior.
I be Pen
My Pen Be ME

I Writes

Scrolled as our Declaration of Presence
I AM HERE
WE ARE HERE

Exertion of permanence
In the nows & ever afters
THIS magic transcends the physical,
And is destined to be imbibed

Get drunk off this immaculately harvested wine
Drink me with your eyes
With your ears

Feel the consonants graze your lips
Bro-Ken Syl-La-Bles ride the wave of that tickled tongue
That stays yearning
Reluctantly
Sheepishly

Metaphors bumrush past gritted teeth
Travel through mouth, seeking throat
Salivate
Getting wet without even trying

Descend into belly
Getting you open from a closed inside
Never knowin' you could
feel
so
full

THEY CALL ME "POETRY"

They call me "The Word Prophet"
Spitting Lines precise like Green Lasers
You'll pay hundreds for front row listening to my fiascoes & frescos
Never wanting to miss the essence of the Spectacular –
May it Never Cease to Exist

They call me "The Syllable Assassin"
Cut-ting IT UP and
Dish-ing IT OUT
Hot? Cold? Lukewarm?
However You Like... WHATEVER You Like
I'll make it sound JUST Right – Served to Order

They call me "The Werrd Smith"
Crafting Lyrical Lesions with the
Expertise of a Surgeon
Scalpel is My Pen
Paper Be the Body
Executing Incisions of Exactness – Line by Line, Stanza by Stanza

They call me "Wordsworth"
Chisel Timeless Poetic Vibes in Stone
Like Etchings of Old,
My Words intrigue, haunt & linger timelessly
As a scalding branding iron emblazons the skin
Flesh blisters with Passion
For the Phonemes of Prose

Roots

The smell of café con leche takes me back to my childhood
Reminds me of Mami getting up, ready to start the new day –
Crisp & rich, just like the coffee she stirred...
Just like her voice...

"Ya es hora de levantarse, Mija"
The taste of arroz con dulce makes me smile
Time travels me to simple days when worries of
who liked who better could be gently eased away with a spoonful
of crema, canela & raisins -
Reminders that sweetness lingers & resonates
from the Inside Out

"Te he dicho, Hija - *Sola la hago, Y Sola la Pago*", Mami'd say
time & time again
Do it for Ourselves, Earn it for Ourselves
Tenemos que hacer nuestra realidad –
Nunca dejes que alguien te diga lo que puedes o no puedes hacer

Somos El Arco Iris entre las nubes
Break away to the shouts of "Azucarrrrrrr!!!" resonating en la cocina
No short supply of sweetener here!
Just the cries of Friday night fiestas in Tia's house
Adonde toda la familia got their salsa on cada fin de semana
Channeling their inner Celia & Tito, con "un chin" del Canario
No birthday, No problema
Vamos a celebrar con mucho "Salud, Dinero Y Amorrrrrrrrrrrrr!!!"

Ridin' down the rumblin' tracks of the 4 & the 6
The epic voyage into El Barrio to visit mis abuelos -
Where the epic love story of mis padres began

Refusing to sit, instead choosing to kneel on the train seat
I peer out its window, with the occasional head nod and shoulder pops
To the booming system,
With Young Pro Ski Wild-Style bumping LL on his radio
Mami, letting Me Be, pero nunca quitándome el ojo de encima -
I watched the tatted subway cars that zoomed past the opposite side
Tryna read the bubble letter tags
Decipher the lines
Glean the messages
Unlock the hierarchical codes -
Catching glimpses of the urban castles that littered the landscape
Catching glimpses of Myself reflected in the flecks of sunshine
that danced on those hazy windows

El aroma de aceite y ajo penetrated your nostrils
as soon as you came up to 116th
We could never just walk past the cuchifrito spot without buying
some alcapurrias y rellenos de papa
Fried to golden perfection, sitting in its lightbulb spotlight
in the window
For the hungry passerby to be mesmerized by
the potential of its saborrrrr...
Welcoming the taste of the sizzle & sting

Todavía lo puedo escuchar...
The crackling of flames on glowing candlewicks
Burning beneath the altar of Abuela's santos in her bedroom
I imagined myself within the glow –
An ember levitating towards the heavens,
Free of restraint -
Gaining strength and Brilliance the higher I float

Caressed and cradled by The Father's calloused Hands,
Doves ruffled in advance to be prepared in the likelihood that
We were made to fall
We still rejoiced in the turbulent flight
Seeing the char in our bones
Singed brows, Sweat-stained & Tear-soaked wings -
Yet, ever ready to attempt achieving new heights once more

And so I grew up.
Learning how & when to place my offering,
Allowing los espíritus to light my way -
Because, now, within these reveries is that I realize
From within the crackle is
Where this Puerto Rican girl was made

Jessica Diaz

Stare

Quiet, Masterful
Scrutinized from tip-to-toe
Inquisitive eyes

Soy / Somos

Déjame decirte quien soy -

Hija de isla Borinqueña, del Encanto
y ciudad y concreto
Nacida de mi arco, Iris
Acariciada con esponjas y brillo
Para ablandarme y endurecerme al mismo tiempo
desarrollada en las buenas y en las malas
extraña como un solo mango entre medio de una palmera de cocos
Vibrante y jugosa con una abundancia de dulzura
Para esos que tienen el corazón para escalar esta altura
Para esos que me muerdan bien

Nacida desde el crucifijo - centrada, simétrica, angulada
Pero con muchas curvas, continuada
Consistentemente fuera del movimiento estructurado
Rumbeando caderas
Rompiendo cintura
Pies descalzos masajeando nuestra tierra
Apoyando las flores que crecen por medio de estos dedos en mis pies

Siempre con buen apetito
Llena de dientes
Devorando de la vida completa
Cojiendo mi tiempo para masticar, contemplar
Saboreando cada momento
porque nunca se sabe si siempre vamos a tener
oportunidad para comer
Cada esfuerzo bien hecho
Corazones contentos y barrigas llenas de buen provecho

Bien sazonados
Mezcal de sal, arena, Bacardi o Don Q
Abrazado con limón
Un pasito atrás, con tres pasitos pa'lante
Este alma gigante
Cojiendo todo este espacio,
Elefante

Tremenda en alma
Agarrando mis sentimientos en estas dos manos
Llena de nuestros recuerdos y oliendo de sus esperanzas

Desde la cultura de mis libros y los bochinches bodegueros
Los cuentos de abuelos y los suspiros de sus espíritus

Soy hija de dos
Madre a millones
Amor por montones
Tratando, sea lo que sea, a manejar esta vida
Que no tiene mapa directa para mujeres
Como Yo

I Am / We Are

Let me tell you who I be -

Daughter of the island Borinqueña,
of Enchantment
And cityscapes & concrete
Birthed from my Rainbow
Caressed with sponges and brillo
To soften me and toughen me up at the same time
Nurtured in the good and the bad
Strange
Like a single mango in a palm tree filled with coconuts
Vibrant & juicy
Abundant in my sweetness -
For those who have the heart to climb these heights
For those who have the teeth to bite into me

Birthed from the crucifix -
Centralized, Symmetrical, Angled
But with plenty of curves
Consistently out of alignment with the expectations of structured
movements
Shaking hips and winding waists
With bare feet massaging the earth I stand on
Supporting the flowers that grow between my toes

Always maintaining a hearty appetite
Full of teeth
Devouring life in its entirety on the daily
Taking my time to chew,
To contemplate
Savoring every moment
Because we never know if we will always have enough to eat
Each struggle endured with precision -
Hearts filled with happiness
Stomachs filled with joy

Well-seasoned
Mixed with salt, sand, Bacardi or Don Q
Hugged in lemon-lime
Singular setbacks with three steps forward in the comeback
This soul be giant
Taking up all this space
With an elephant-sized grace

Full of Spirit
Holding onto my feelings within these 2 hands
Filled with our memories, and the lingering aroma of our hopes

From the culture of our books and our bodega gossip
From grandparents' old tales and the exhales of their spirits

I am the daughter of two
Mother to millions
Love by the ton
Trying my best to steer this life
That doesn't seem to have a direct map for women
Like Me

TRESSES

the Outsiders trying to convince us
to denounce the blessing

The Blessing of the:

     Coily
         Kinky
     Curly
         Frizzy
     Coarse
         Unruly

Blatantly Rebellious -
Goading eyes to stare

Tempting hands to -
Touch
Caress
Fondle its curves

Bold & Brazen -
Flashes of golden sun rays beam through the cascades of
     Auburns
         &
     Browns
         & Ochres

Willful -
Of its own body and mind
Her audacity,
Playfully taunting the voluminous skies
Slyly pondering to herself:
Should I be shy & submissive today?
Or, roar wildly as the Queen Lioness?
Dispersing vibes like electromagnetic undulations
of sensory power

Is there even a decision to be made here?

Vibrant & Spirited
She is.
...Though such has not always been the case.
This dandelion has roughed journeys
Several a windstorm in this past
But,
        In actuality,
Dandelion seeds still tumultuously continue to be
        Scattered
                To & fro

At times -
Aimless

At times -
Quite direct

Purposeful.
Seemingly Visionary.

Can you believe that?
Can she be the best kept secret in plain sight?

Hold steadfast to the waves,
Be they unconventional, to them

Alluring
     Intoxicating
Enterprising
     Fascinatinating

Juxtaposed with -
     Fear
        Intimidation
     Subjugation
        Despise & Loathing

From without,
Even from within...
The War of Rages continues on.

Maybe an eternal fight...
To tame or not to tame?

    Should this even be a question?

Dimming shine to quell the Outsiders insecurities
In relation to maintaining the "status quo"?
Maintaining "order"?
Preserving "normalcy"?

Question needs to be:
To whom?
For whom?
By whom?

The ancestors beg of you -
Be clear in your thinking of this
Whose purpose are we serving?

So just as Night falls upon its Mother,
Its back becoming one with her Earth cradle
I now give my tresses the same permission -

To intermingle
To reside openly
To unravel
To take up space unapologetically
To rest easy in her Black & Taino

Just as the blissful blades of grass lovingly embrace Night
I now hug the roots generously granted unto me
Each curl a Blackfisted portrait of ancestral legacy
Unable to be erased regardless of applied heat

Melding as one -
As was begun
As will continue
As was meant to be

Truth is realized
Subtlety injected into me within each sun ray
Captured and multiplied within each rizo

Happyness is birthed from the root

The ancestors beg of you -
Unearth it.

Keep digging

FaCed

Look at me
Outfitted faces
Layered upon layered upon layered
Melding the core
Am I wearing it, or is it wearing me?

Temporary facades fabricated in vain
Attempts to ease,
Sustain pain
Hide fragile frames

Disguised from the fates
Disguised from perception
But, eventually,
Ethereal intervention always allows for true
Reflection

The distinct intersection where mask fuses to flesh
Under hushed breath
Fearful to reveal the truth of its connection

Yet, be contented!
Being Me - in the truest sense
Multifaceted
Multidimensional
Recognize the LeVeLs to this
Affirmative - my actions been from the onset
Despite the veil that once shrouded self-doubt

Let it be the false ones to make contradictions,
Trying to convince us to shield our radiant visage

Crush the seemingly almighty masquerade!
Watch this curtsey as I plant my crown upon this whimsied mane of
cheeried locks

Focused gaze through feathered lashes and
Signature elongated lash line

I shout confidently until I have no choice but to
Be that which I had feigned

  - Extracted
  - Attracted
  - Refracted

  Light Source

FaCed -
Tetrahedrons
Poly-he-drawn my several faces
Existential places
Co-existing as the visible & invisible
When eye see fit

Ghosting into present image
Becoming who I decide to be
Coming in & out of view as I please
Maintain my constance
Embody that legacy

Mask evolves to mirror
Constructed from the shards of multi-colored mosaic'ed glass
fragments
Of the past lives of my sistren
reflecting my fates from which destiny will never escape

I am fused
No hollowed mask
No hyding here.

Look at me -
Holistic revelation

El Peleador Callejero

Enrutado
    con
  movimientos
        descalzos

Pero

    FIRMES.

Esos pies han caminado sobre todo

A los riesgos del corazón,
Él se le rie

Sabiendo que - sea lo que sea -

LA LUCHA SIEMPRE TRAE SATISFACCIÓN.

Entrenado
    para mover

        montañas, y después

Darle unos pasos a la Salsa en Celebración

Bruto para los que no sepan,
pero
este hombre
si se la sabe
todo

Comiendo mentiras por desayuno desde niñez
Su alimento para sobrevivir en Las Calles

      Las Calles que se le pusieron al frente,
                y por encima

Pelear no fue una reacción
Más un recuerdo de quien sus padres eran

Y COMO EL RESPETO TIENE QUE ESTAR EXIGIDO
EN LA VIDA.

Piel canela con
sus chispas de

          Fuego y Oro

        Caliente y Brillante

        Lleno de energía

      para EXISTIR.

The Street Fighter

Routed
      With
    barefooted
              movements

But

      FIRM.

Those feet have walked over everything

To the risks of the heart,
He laughs at Her
Knowing that - whatever it is -

THE FIGHT ALWAYS BRINGS SATISFACTION.

Trained
        to move
                  mountains, and after

Take a few steps to Salsa in Celebration

Grotesque simpleton, for those who do not know
but
this man
knows
everything

Eat-ing lies for break-fast since his child-hood
Lies be his food to survive in these streets

The streets that were put in front of him,
and upon him

Fighting was not a reaction
But a memory of who his parents were and how

RESPECT HAS TO BE DEMANDED IN THIS LIFE.

That cinnamon skin
with its sparks of

Fire and Gold

Hot and Shiny

Holding full energy

to EXIST.

Who's Bitch?

"Hey, Bitch!"
BIG BITCH / little bitch
Weak Bitch
BAAD BITCH
Whack Bitch
BOSS Bitch
lazy bitch
Rich Bitch
Broke Bitch
Smart Bitch
Dumb bytch
Ho Bitch
Sneaky Bitch
Thot Bitch
Nosey Bitch
His Bitch
Her Bitch
Your Bitch
They Bitch
This Bitch
That Bitch
Our Bitch
My Bitch.
Yo, Bitch!?!

What's the matter?
What's in a word?
Why the concern?

NEVER would I claim a name that
Degrades my frame of mind, my existence
Of pertinence
Of resilience

Dethrone myself of my Queendom, or
Let another snatch it?
Not havin' it.

As abrupt and as disrespectful as it sounds
Monosyllabic label with infinite repercussions
Sparking never-ending discussions as to what it should or should not
mean
As abrupt and as disrespectful as its intention

Spilled from a voicebox detached from sensibility
Why would I enable you, let you attach this to me?

Does my realness scare you?

Attempts at belittlement
Infection of one's self perception
Is this fear evoked because of insecurity?
Sense of inferiority?
Egocentric need to activate hypermasculinity?

Let the record show that I as all of Shes
are birthed in testosterone too

Don't undermine my ability to make a bitch outta you

FERTILE

Creation
The motivation of every living being
To create legacy
To impact destiny
To be more than an occasional warbled murmur in an ill-recalled
memory
Made to birth another to continue to grow the tale, enhance the
Earth's story
To breed, and proceed to give more life once more

But, dare I ask:
Is the only way to see this goal met through the action of fornication,
unprotected sex?

Cuz I been birthing more than a life in all of my years
Don't worry about my ovaries
Dis pen be just as fertile
Ink droplets fertilized by the X's & Y's, all consonants & vowels
Mother to my syllables, and sonnets, free verses and hot barz on all topics

Societal norms casting love spells that bound hearts
and minds to the fallacy
That the only way woman can be fulfilled is through pregnancy
A life sans children be not one to call
A scarlet branding of defect, of wanton neglect
Female psyche conditioned to tread lightly on this crazy notion
that they can actually decide which cards they want dealt, and when

But, dare I ask:
Is woman less if she chooses to decide otherwise? Like our male
counterparts have had the luxury to do throughout time?

Cuz I been birthing more than a life in all of my years
Don't worry about my ovaries
Dis pen be just as fertile
Ink droplets fertilized by the X's & Y's, all consonants & vowels
Mother to my syllables, and sonnets, free verses and hot barz on all topics

Defective
Lack of seedlings, of multiple Mini-Me's by the age of 33
Leading to automatic assumptions of biological deficiency
Something's wrong with She -
"Poor thing, how sad that she doesn't have any..."
"Such a lovely woman..."
"Pity she won't be able to share that beauty with progeny..."
Smarts & talent unable to be nurtured in her babies

But, dare I ask:
If biologically procreation is not a possibility, should that not just be
accepted as this woman's path as meant to be?

Cuz I been birthing more than a life in all of my years
Don't worry about my ovaries
Dis pen be just as fertile
Ink droplets fertilized by the X's & Y's, all consonants & vowels
Mother to my syllables, and sonnets, free verses and hot barz on all topics

Full of all the -ishes,
She is instantaneously labeled
Even before getting 4 words out of her mouth at the red table
"My Body, My Choice" -
Translates to Self-ishness
Met with the astonished gaze of mother, father, sister, brother,
aunties and uncles and cousins and WHOEVER else can get within
earshot of this deemed "freakish" perception -
When a woman dares to want it all in life, minus conception

But, dare I ask:
What is the tragedy in trusting a woman's judgment? Is she tarnishing the
sanctity of other's motherhood if she does this?

Cuz I been birthing more than a life in all of my years
Don't worry about my ovaries
Dis pen be just as fertile
Ink droplets fertilized by the X's & Y's, all consonants & vowels
Mother to my syllables, and sonnets, free verses and hot barz on all topics

No stress, I'll be that -ish
Roguish to the supposed Standard,
Traditional thoughts of what I dare not miss
I will not punish myself for checking "other"
I will not be vanquished, labeled as odd
Because the contractions I chose to endure are the ones I sprinkle
throughout my sentences
I'm still a woman
I'll impact the world with this Life that is mine
My womanhood is not defined by my reproductive organs
productivity

So don't you dare ask me about my damn ovaries! -
Cuz I been birthing more than a life in all of my years
Dis pen stays fertile
Ink droplets fertilized by the X's & Y's, all consonants & vowels
Mother to my syllables, and sonnets, free verses and hot barz on all topics

I be Full & Finished
Complete & Polished
Brimming with Light & Promise
Worthy & Established in my Own Right
Birthing Dreams & Possibilities
Everytime this woman chooses to write

In This Body

Happiness lives in this body
Residing in various timeshares throughout the year
She has a traveler's spirit
Adventurous
Tapping into different corners,
Warming herself in various ways
Happiness naps in my ears
Finding peace in being massaged by music's soundwaves
Finding her center when silence tippy toes in to kiss her forehead
Happiness sings in my arms
Sometimes operatic - Firm. Convincing. Protective.
Sometimes as a lullaby - Soft. Vulnerable. Naked.
Hugs giving and receiving love
Reciprocity
Coming full circle

Battle: COVID-19 Versus BX 1

Intrusion –
This false illusion that you JUST stepped up on the block in March
FARCE.
What? - You lookin' at me wit da side-eye...
Tryna say I'm lyin'?
Or, are you just surprised that I know the definition?

Ain't nuttin' new to dis
You've been scheming,
Stay feenin'
To infect these Bronx Streets further
Tryna hurt da Little Ones we got that we're grooming to come up

Nah, you done picked the wrong ones, Yo

Hypervigilant
Indiscriminate
Any of Yah can get these hands –
SARS – EBOLA – H1N1
COVID – MORBID?
Ha, Kid... You gon REALLY be in for it

Done seen your attempts to keep us hidden
Lack of funding
keepin' us wonderin:
Is the next check comin'?
Will our businesses be reopenin'?
Is this my last day breathin'?

Socioeconomic Status -
The apparatus that
keeps Us unable to know IF We even Have THIS?

Jessica Diaz

Ain't nuttin' nice about being considered last
For everything else
But, being the #1 in zip codes grapplin' wit dis shit

BUT, we gon' Be Alriiight.

Let me tell you what it be -
The strongest ALWAYS get hit hardest
Cuz they wanna test these styez
So, show 'em...

Let em know how:
Our rhymez be limitless
Vibrations cause the synthesis of
Positive energies that be birthed from this uterus
Head-to-Head, Toe-to-Toe –
How we doin' this?

Highly infectious, Reckless
This fiyah I'm spittin'
Brazen
Did I done left you breathless?

I see you backing up off me
Dat's right, B
6 feet or betta, Neva let up
Hit you wit this 1-2 Mortal Kombat move
----- Can ya get up?

Still spittin', Your flinchin'
Don't like the feelin' of me breachin' your Social Distancin'?

PANDEMIC, yeah the World said it
But, trust & believe, you gon' get wetted
We been preppin' for dis battle – EPIC.

Masked vigilante,
Come get at We
I blast thee wit dis
Anti-
Virus... Probe your sinus
Inject our slyness
When you thought you were da one creepin' up behind us

Rockin' yo bells like LL
Grip the mic tight
You really believe you can last 12?

You'll spiral as we go viral
Backhand slapping' ya like ol' skool mamas do
Rootin' ourselves on cuz we know no one else gon do

Antibodies hood-strong
We done punked you
Microscopic or not, you gon' get got

Sleepin' on us
'Rona, please – We never sleep
Stay grindin', Hustle harder – HARDEST
Inflict you with the awe of our marvelousness
Leave you hurtin'
Skirtin' that you 'fraid of us
Knowin' our untapped potential be endless,
Leaving you lifeless –
Tapped out. Push this, too, behind us.

We lean on da homies for our resolutions
Ears to da street, Scoutin' for our next opportunity Al-Rea-DY
Easing our Peeples' pains like EX-Ce-De-Rin
Better den - Us?
Be. No. Other.

WE Rise up and take it
CHANGE IT.
It be Us, the Agents – the Artists – the Educators
Infiltrate the Systems
Saliva droplets ricochet off our mics, our pages
Graffiti scrolls timelining our Majors
Each Teachin' the Stories of Our Ages, and how the battle must
continue on
We so bright, the foes will continue to step tah us
That's why we ALWAYS gotta be prepared to knuckle up
In this Cryptic Break---

Dance Apocalyptic
Review their scripted trajectories for Us and
REVISE IT.
We didn't hire the DJ at this particular house party
But, we gotz the records, the histories...
And we done never turned down a battle before.
Replace the needle. Flip the vinyl.
Drop our beat,
and Scratch. The Fuck. ON.

White-Washed: Graffiti's Exclusive Interview

I'm not invisible
Call me Ms. Invincible.
My movements been rooted in the dome like the instinctual
Fueling this fire we seek since Being was in utero

"A different Animal, but the same Beast" –
Like Yeezy inviting all daring spectators to come take a peek

Don't dare call me by your government's names –
Urban Decay
Topographic Terrorism
Utter Vandalism
Straight Trash
Address me accordingly! You know you see this majestic mane –
"Your Highness… They await you."
- When "The Ruler" speaks, wait your turn and listen for the
breakthrough
Hear me speak; but can you bear to hear

Not quite the open metaphorical book
But, put in that werk
Reach high upon these shelves
Clutch my spine
Turn my pages
Sift through my many incarnations
Read me. Feel me.
No classical labels
No big institution stables
- Just beaming colors & curves
Slick wit tha werd, and a passion to be heard –
No Pause. Only Push Play, and Repeat.

I be Old Skool roots with New World perspectives
I gets OPEN,
Yet, equally cautious - keeping Our dynamic histories close.

Fearing trusting allowances to bask in our Earthly richness will
prompt Him to appropriate
What is inherently Ours once more

My worth does not lie in your hands, as you've made it seem
THIS Beauty is Epic – lining the urban cityscapes
Reverberations of peeples' voices speaking my name

I spread the Vibe...
Vibrations
Mos Defiantly.
Playing our hood symphonies in audio-less
Vertical / Horizontal manifestations

Not knowing all the answers of what to do
But, it's cool –
It's the questions that guide us anyways
My magic lies in this mosaic'd mess

Self-Identification, proclaiming as:
Ms. Multi-Cultural
Ms. Multi-Faceted
Ms. Multi-Disciplinary

Yet, STILL branded as:
Miss Understood
Miss Represented
Miss Communicated

But, like I said – It's cool...

Not waiting on Him to deem me priceless
Our inner value is limitless.
Motivations and Movements, Pure of Heart
As we hold true to remain this bold spectrum of Outlaw Art

Mariposa Negra

Intentaron llamarme la oveja negra
Marcándome con sus maldiciones
Categorizándome como otra
empujándome al rebaño
dejándome sin rumbo
sin propósito ni dirección
Pero tuve que mostrarles que no tengo nada de oveja
mas que este pelo rizado -
Mi halo dotado de historia, poder y grandeza
Suave, grueso y fino *a la misma vez*
La joya escondida, gema oculta
Siempre me querían tocar
¿Cómo si ellos pudieran manejarme? Capturarme?
Creyéndose dueños de esta finca que llamamos sociedad
Se niegan a admitir que ningunas manos blancas pueden
Crear una magia como este
Que tengo encima de mi y por dentro *a la misma vez*
Trataron quitarnos nuestra luz, nuestro fuego, nuestra visión
Pero descubrieron rápidamente que este animal es libre

Bautizada y bendecida por las manos negras de mis ancestros
dedos fuertes que pudieron agarrar el sol y exprimir la felicidad fresca
Con unas hechas de estrellas
Revelaron la potencia de nuestras tierras
Unas sucias, pero orgullosas *a la misma vez*
Que con su relámpagos revivieron mi espíritu del sueño
Usando las penas y tristezas de la luna para crearme en una nueva
esperanza
Esas manos prepararon la tierra con sus sabores, sus labores
Sus cuentos caseros y historias antiguas
Tierra llena de dulce y sal
Inundada con agua de caña y de coco
Y con sangre y sudor
Para ahogarme y refrescarme *a la misma vez*

Desde esta abundancia, esencia de agrio y dulzura
es que yo comi
Comiendo por la boca
Lambiendo el camino con mis pies
Saboreando de la naturaleza de mis orígenes
Llenándome
Engordándome
Relambiendome, lista para hartarme de paciencia y fe
Preparándome para mi destino
Segura de mi vuelo -
Acordándome de nuestras penas y nuestras alegrías *a la misma vez*
Reclamando mi nombre como yo lo me merezco
Como es debido
Esta Mariposa Negra -
Reconocida y escondida *a la misma vez*
No se te olvides que
Para salir del cascarón tuve que poner mis fuerzas
Alas en multitud
Echándole ganas a mis muchas paradas
No me puedes matar
Solamente me pongo a dormir
Para reanimarme y dar a luz a nuestra existencia eterna

Alas negras absorbiendo todo este sol
Siendo codiciosas pero generosas *a la misma vez*
Me las puede mirar con admiración o con celo
Pero nunca va cambiar que son mías de todo derecho
Sosteniendo las riquezas del universo en cada membrana
Mal de ojos no pueden pegarse a esta furia de colores
Cada capa reflejando a otra lucha superada
Sorprendido que mis alas pueden apartar el viento de su camino
Cuando se creyeron que ellos gobernaron el aire también
Alas delicadas pero robustas *a la misma vez*
Me han dejado huellas

Pero animales como yo no se asustan tan fácil
Se dice que: "El que tenga miedo de morir que no nazca"
Pues, nosotros nos moriremos un poco a cada amanecer
Para seguir disfrutando del placer de vivir y superar
en nuestra imagen
Sin preocupación cuánto se tarda
Siempre llegare
Libres, sin disculpas
Volando nuestras queridas rutas

Black Butterfly

They tried to call me the Black Sheep
Branding me with their curses
Categorizing me as "Other"
pushing me into the flock
Leaving me aimless
without purpose or direction
But I had to show them that there ain't nothing
Sheepish about me except the texture of this curly hair -
My halo is endowed with history,
power and greatness
Soft, thick and fine *at the same time*
The hidden gem, obscured jewel
They always wanting to touch me
As if they could handle me? Capture me?
Believing themselves owners of this farm we call Society
They refuse to admit that no white hands can
Create magic like this
Magic bathed on my skin and sweatin' out my pores *at the same time*
They tried to take away our light, our fire, our vision.
But they quickly discovered that this animal is free.

ÓYEME

Baptized and blessed by the Black hands of my ancestors
Strong fingers that could grab the sun
to produce fresh-squeezed happiness
With fingernails made of stars
They revealed the power of our lands
Dirty fingernails, but filled with pride *at the same time*
Their lightning hearts revived my spirit from their wildest dreams
Using their moon-shadowed hurts and sorrows
to create me in a new hope
Those hands prepared the land with their flavas, their labors
With countryside tall tales and wise words
from their mama's mamas mamas
Land full of saccharin and salt
Flooded with sugarcane and coconut water
And with blood and sweat
To drown me and cleanse me *at the same time*

From this abundance,
essence of sour and sweetness is that I eat
Feeding my mouth
Licking pathways clean with my ordained feet
Savoring the nature of my Origins
Filling me up
Getting phat
Lickin' my lips, ready to get gorged with patience and faith
Preparing for my destiny
Safely secured for my flight -
Remembering our sorrows and our joys at the same time
Reclaiming my name because I deserve it,
As it should be.

This Black Butterfly -
Easily recognized and overtly hidden at the same time
Don't forget that to get out of that shell I had to go in full-strength
Wingspeed on overdrive
Facing forward with confidence despite my many stops
You can't kill me
I just go to sleep
To regenerate and give birth
to our eternal ancestral existence once more

Black wings absorbing all this sun
Being greedy but generous *at the same time*
You can look at them with admiration or jealousy, whichever you'd like
But it will never change the fact that they are rightfully mine
Holding the riches of the Universe in every membrane
Evil eyes cannot stick to this fury of colors
Each layer reflecting another struggle overcome
Surprised that my wings can keep the wind out of their way
When They believed that they ruled the air too
Wings, delicate but robust *at the same time*
Welts don't go away, they've left their traces on me

But animals like me don't get scared easily
It is said that: "He who is afraid of dying let him not be born"
Well, we will die a little at every dawn then
To continue enjoying the pleasure of living and overcoming
With no worries about how long it takes
We'll always arrive
Free, No Apologies
Navigating our own desired routes

Bronx Girls

(Inspired by "Silent Killa" aka "Supreme Tigress" - Tanika)

Within the rattles & hums, booms & bips of the borough
Lie the silence(hers)...

Deadlier than a gun and its pop
Because we go unseen & unheard
Underestimation is our weapon of choice,
And we learn early how to use this camouflage to finish them

To that chick that runs dolo -
Her mind is right,
And so are these hands -
Choose how you gonna get em by the way you step
So come correct, or not at all

With origins in tha werd;
But unapologetic   when having to
    break
        the line
            To get a [.]
   across

Carving intricate plots on how to change the world,
One hood at a time -
With the architecture of her mind
The flows of her wines
Intermingled with the knowledge of self & thine

Unpolished, like the grainy underside of a firmly seated pearl
She cleans up nice
Always shining, even when closed for self-preservation
Muting all reservation of lack of greatness
When she opens up to flash her smile
Those eyes been birthed out of heavy love
And laid on low expectation,
Toiling generations to paint a realer image of what
It's really like to be us
Holding on to her truth
Untethered to stereotype
Cocoa-buttered realness
With proud dangling hoops for days,
With wise-assness being her favorite game to play

Heavy crowns are most comfortable on the head of royalty
So this noun bestows upon herself the proper prefix,
Ms. Extra-ordinary -
From tha baddest, to the gooder, to The Great
These Bronx girls -
They just ain't made the same.

Taste of Native Tongues *(inspired by Bronx y Nuyorican Flavas)*

If I had no tongue
I'd learn to taste this life with my feets
Toes lickin' concrete
Cada dedo relamiéndose porque le gustan los dulces duros
Each paso sopping up da buttamilk beats of these streets
Cuz we alls about a good biscuit, ya heard?

Mmmmmm, can you smell that?
That's my Hood's Gumbo stewing, brewing
Hecho en los calderos de nuestras abuelas y bisabuelas
Bubblin' up la salsa, soul, hip hop y cumbias
That rumble through sound systems, and veins
Every Saturday morning cuando la gente se ponen a mover
las caderas, y sus escobas
Ese asopao calentandose, waiting patiently to be devoured by its
Natives
Bellies attentive, vibin' with the aroma
Cuz we ain't neva been scared to seek out what's rightfully meant for
us to eat

Ingest & digest this stewpot of mixed ingredients
Where herbs, spices and condiments are married with
Grit, guttural passion and killah instincts
An urban sofrito of sorts que siempre se deja comer
And even if I had no tongue to taste it, no importa
Because flava this strong goes beyond the tongue's pitted surface
Nuestro sabor is rooted in bone, skeletal
Como el hueso de vaca entre ese mismo asopao

Feeding my soul through my soles
As I walk these Bronx streets
Taking big bites from the culture
That willingly & lovingly serves it up to its peoples on the daily
Brick walls serving as silver platters
Offering its residents delectable delicacies
Carved and seasoned and displayed
In the most diverse arrays of shapes, colors and bubble letters
Welcoming all to servierse un plato
Chewin' on graf like Starbursts
I be tastin' tha rainbow in the sights & sounds of this often tragically
misunderstood place
Champion borough,
Burrowed in equal parts de amargura y dulzura at times
Pero todo bien cool cuz there's beauty in that too
And that's why they gotta put respekt on our name with a "The"
Cuz ain't no place like it
Ain't no place like home

So I chew slowly on each mouthful
Swallow all of its marred ego and charm

Gulp
Belly full

Suffocate

Tight Grip
Fingerprints still visible on my skin
No meds can release the tension surrounding my esophagus
Windpipe restricted, as my voice becomes less & less audible
Pallor envelops me as my body proceeds to collapse

No air
No words

But, even though sound has escaped me,
My thoughts still exist.

Maybe you think you can lower my volume
Lessen this frequency
Obstruct my words

But, never can you slay my thoughts

Heart & Mind stay strong
FEARLESS

Always resilient in withstanding your grip

Choke on that.

Oye, Nena...
(Aviso Número Dos De Mama)

Esos nombres que te llaman ahora:
Nerdy
Gordita
Quiet
Will be your greatness one day
Ya tú veras
Nerdiness makes you money, honey
Y los comentarios que "estás gordita"
Van a cambiarse a: *¡Mami, tú sí estás dura!*
Al príncipe que te merezca
And being quiet
Eso te hace observadora
You'll be able to spot the bullshit from a mile away
And avoid las jodiendas de la gente,
Esas voces negativas no sirven en tu vida

What I Love Most

What I Love Most?...
I love that one tendril of auburn hair
You know… The one that never fails to remind me of what the
PLAN IS
And, thennnnnn, that which what REAALLLY Happens
The one that never knew how to ride the straight line of a hot comb
Light as air - TWISSSSTYYYY
Whimsical & Sweet
Like ruffled socks taggin' along on Buster Brown'ddd feets -
Hopscotching & Double-dutching in these streetzzzz
Young, Yet wise in these Games
She be knowin' the rhythms and flows of which she's been ordained
to go
Trusting in the hood's beats, the hot 16's, the barzzzz that
intermingle within each
and everrry single, solitary strand on this head:
HARD
DENSE
TEXTURED
LAYERED…
And LOVIN' how once you've been gripped in it,
Neither He, She, They or Them can seem to let go
Stone-Cold frozen in its gaze
Misrepresented Medusa
Getting a bad wrap about what these tresses actually do
Swatting away envies like flies off shhhhhhhifty individuals
Each day the mane is awakened in new freedoms,
With transformation and elevation locked into each curl

What I Love Most?...
I love eyelashes that curve to the Heavens, waving happily as I bow
down and pray
Downward doggin'
Greeting the ancestors and joining them in prayer as they bless my
future tomorrows

Unified front in protecting these eyes whose sights must remain clear
To continue the journey that those ancestors tagged her into -
to relay, to continue
Batting angelic wings
Holding tight to these innervisions
Hopes & Dreams being more than just Hopes & Dreams
Rather more Truths & Triumphs
Discoveries & Revelations
The Will Be's & Must-Haves
The path is for me to see and traverse
So I hold steady gaze to this verse
As I wink flirtatiously to those naysayers who count me out
"Wait til they get a load of me"
Clueless, never understanding that I ain't built to bow out
*Wink wink

What I Love Most?...
That hard slope of a nose bridge,
Seemingly simple with no reason or purpose but
To BE
Yet, quite contrary
as it provides the pathway for that one bead of sweat that appears -
CENTERED.
CASCADING & CLEANSING,
CARESSING and TRACING its way to the tip
Providing a physical place to hold just barely a droplet of all this
magic
that churns within'
and gracefully condenses out
Doubling as the landing strip for My Love's lips and whiskers
Kissing the symmetry of my face -
The literal center of my Left and my Right
Acknowledging that the truest and gentlest and kindest of Love
Always is rooted in the center
Demarcating the straight route to my mouth
Always in alignment with the whimsies and introspections of
this brain

Pulling Neos
Bending time
Scrimpin' & Scrapin'
Snatchin' back what's been mines
Be it through the laborious physical grind or the constant exercising
of the academic muscle
She hustles
The toil is real
As straight-laced and composed as she may seem
Know that the price for remaining stoic isn't cheap, or easy
Particularly when it appears as if the whole world is staring,
just waiting for her to show she's weak
But, again, holdin' it together
By any means
Blood, sweat & tears all have rented space on this brow, this face
Push forward, tapped into my spiritual place
Because we be knowing of nothin' else
Continuing to unleash our magic in spite of revisionist history
Licking my lips, tasting the beads
Salty yet surprisingly sweet
Because the grind is hard,
but hearty in what it reaps

What I Love Most?...
This voice
Aggressively Invading Mental Space
Sprinkled with some special
Sound captured in iridescent soap-filmed bubbles, attempting to
escape my throat
DELICATE
MAJESTIC
Encapsulated with purpose
Poppin' at the drop of a hat, or the flip of a coin
Forcing them to See the magic in Me
The Bronx is Breathing In these lungs,
sustaining the werd fueled by the herd
as we graze in our own homegrown sustenance
We giving the werd its flowers while it's still here

Voice be soothin'
Trancing
Instant state to meditate, help mediate the drama
No need to self-medicate
The lines I spit be way more than enough to get ya high off tha vibez
No need to pump up the volume
Voice be boomin' factuals and actuals
Teaching ya'll that being loud don't make you right...
Funny how the subtlest of lines can make you think twice?

What I Love Most?...
that Conscious & Unconscious Mind
Outsleeping the Sun
Playing tag with the Moon
Drinking in the White Noise
Breathing out galaxies of stars
Living in Midnight, and in Lullabies
Chewing slow on the memories that surface in slumber
Savory and full of spice
Hands outstretched, landingstrips for my blessings
Clenched fists needed no more as the dark omens dispel
In this sanctuary of cerebrum
Imagination takes flight
Direction is limitless, Opportunities a plenty
Left & Right interlock fingers, officially announcing their coupling
Left-Brain letting go of the supposed correct calculation
of the equation
Giving in to Right-Brain's analog clock
Following those creative ticks that surprisingly elevate
the educative niche
Empowering the spin of axis
Deconstructing praxis
Educating, Closing Gapsss iz
What this mind was made to do

What Do I Love Most?...
Damn, Let me love up on all of this YOU

CHAPTER 2

Oye, Nena…
(Aviso Número Tres De Mama)

La vida es una
Y Dios ve todo
Las bendiciones y los mal de ojos
Tenga fe y ponle atención a esos instintos
Porque esas sensaciones no son un accidente
Ni una exageración de la imaginación
Esos son sus ángeles guardianas
Sutilmente dándote consejos

The "In-Between"

I gotta find the in between, you know
The equilibrium within self-care & poised traction
Symbiotic Reactions
The pushes and pulls that lead to satisfaction
With just the right amount of stop & go
Where my 2 steps forward are always firm

The need in me to succeed
Heeds the calling
The storyteller will always find the means to tell
No fall back, I know that
...But I still don't do early mornings
... and I don't do rise and grinds
I've never risen to seek the worm
I've never been that type of bird

Hunting the words different
I vibe like the owl -
More like a late night and chill
With intense gaze and attuned with piercing silence
With deep reflections and the anticipation of a freshly uncapped pen
Foreplay, as its tip saunters closer
To penetrate the naked page

This is probably what makes this the in between, though
Cuz there's no rewind
Only pause & play
Taking a deep inhale and exhale with
Every letter written and erased
And sometimes we just ain't ready to know
What really happens to the protagonist in the end
Even when the protagonist is you
And you're the only one in charge
Of holding the pen
Of scribing how the story is told
And deciding when to
End

BRAIN CHEMISTRY
(Inspired by the Theory of "Left-Brained" & "Right-Brained" personalities)

Description of "SELF":

I am CENTER -
BOTH Left & Right.

I am the scientist who hears the roaring laughter,
becomes enveloped in the vibrant colors and wiggles my toes
in the sand
But then contemplates -
HOW is this Happening?
What is the magnitude of this experience? Can this be intensified
& replicated?...
Will this moment always be the case?

Can it ever be frozen in time? Or, is it forever fluid?
I am CENTER.
I am Rational, Logical & Accurate in my questioning of Both
the linear, the numerical
AND the creative, the abstract.

I am CENTER -
NO Left or Right.
No Vertical Line can encapsulate the wondrous mechanism of
my brain.
You could, therefore, say I am a Diagonal -
Infinite Possibilities, Absolutely No Boundaries.

Skewed, slanted...
I will never hit the floor, lowest of the low;
Or, hit the ceiling - reaching a cap max to
My Growth,
My Creativity,
My Flow.

Flexible, Ever-Changing...
The Artistic Philosopher.

I Am Center.

I AM SELF.

Illusion

I am in control.
Am I?

Control is an illusion.
Illusion can control who we are when the mask comes off.

Who are we when the masks come off?...
Who does the mask come off of?
Is it by choice or a forceful reveal?
Who will be brave enough to show a bare face
to a judgmental world?

The unmasking can peel some of us too.
Unraveling the tethering can be painful.
But painful doesn't mean unnecessary.

I am in control,
Even as an illusion in the eyes of the naysayers.

My illusion is the control.
Your underestimation is my greatest cover.

Blackberry Woman

Grown from the ancestral crown,
this Lovely Atlas
Heavy be the burdens, but she was built to support this weight
Glory be in her mournings
Regal in carriage even when she's been dusted in loss & regret
Consuming the sun
With equal parts of radiance and heat
Skin shimmering with sweat and loyalty
Exhaling generational traumas and societal deceits
Continuously toiling in a life that constantly tries to strip her
of her sovereignty
Supple to her own trusting touch
But quite prickly to those fingertips that try to grasp at her roughly
Such be the irony -
Admired and desired for the same things that deem her otherly
Aubergine stains long remain on the lips of the loves
Who tried to steal a wisp of her magic
Find healing in her wetness
Feed off the natural saccharine that is harvested in her
arches and curves
Capture the galaxies that lie in those amethyst eyes
Clinging to the forever in a warmth like hers

Just another in the list of things she must do
Attempting to love herself while being overly consumed by you

Lions to Lambs

"Sometimes you have to be a lion so you can be the lamb you really are."

- Yvonne Seon, Dave Chapelle's Mother

Birthed in a different pasture
Yet yearning for the same fruit
Wanting that same feast
Longing for the invitation to the seat

But
Hope be a waitlist
And Quiet don't speak volumes
Patience can't enter the room first
And waiting a turn doesn't exist when yielding only goes left

Safety within the flock is comfortable, instinctual
Cloaked in smokey greys, staying in flow
Following the Leader, as has been told
Because standing apart attracts too much attention
Standing out makes too much noise
Scrutiny, by any means, what we've been made to avoid

But
Vision be a birthright
A Yes spirit ain't born from a Maybe heart
And dreams don't become reality within eternal sleep
Purpose can't graze within groupthink

Shear off that fear masked as safety
Let body be baptized with curiosity
Skin electric as uncertainty dances on skin
Claim space
Roar boisterously so they can hear

No lies - Insecurity be a mutherfucka
So you gotta slap it wit a ya backhand
That way it won't creep
And say it again, again, again and again
Persistence is the fabric of this fresh fleece

That ain't background noise no more
No stutters, No whines, No whispers
That be Promise stepping forth
Feedin' off of the new crops she's layin'
Planting the seeds of elevation
Blooming reminders of our destined creation

Instinct and Life are best friends
We ain't gon lose one if we got each others
Shatterin' those ceilings so all the shawties can have sun

Puzzle pieces neva' just leisurely fall into place
Stress be an annoyin' lil brotha
But, memba', that keen vision ain't neva failin'
Won't be alone just because we are the first
No such thang as selfish when the moves are blazin' a trail
Lead, Baby
                    Let Legacy prevail

Ser Mujer

Ser mujer es ser completa,
no te creas que necesitas del hombre para vivir.
No es posible necesitarlo
cuando son las mujeres las que crean vida.
Ser mujer es ser bendecida,
de este corazón la luz de la existencia nació,
puedes verlo cuando le miras a los ojos,
ojos marrones, negros, azules o verdes;
cada uno reflejando nuestras tierras, naturaleza y cultura.
Nuestros ojos ven todo,
les dan una oportunidad a aquellos que no temen mirarnos
profundamente,
como un hombre suficiente para mantener una mirada firme
y ver un futuro junto a la alegría.
Ser mujer es ser imparable,
Maturada en nuestros vientres y muestreada
en nuestros movimientos,
en cada paso descalzo hacia tus sueños,
en cada toque apasionado cuando luchas por tus metas,
en cada suspiro de tristeza, cansancio o amor.
Exhalando esperanza en medio de la desesperanza,
creando un nuevo camino por donde quiera que vayas,
esto es tu poder.
Ser mujer es ser inexplicable,
te lo mostraré incluso mejor de lo que te puedo decir:
mírame y toma notas.

Tears & Cheek

Play on the "tongue and cheek"
Tears lick my cheeks instead
Learnin' to stop questionin' my fallin'
Rather be joyous that I can still revisit
The feelins' before the fall

Climbin', wellin' up from within
Voyaging beyond the periphery of orbital sins
Tryin' to interpret the withouts
Seeping gradually into the crinkles of self-doubt

Roll through, Roll on, Roll from
Traversing across supple, rose-colored terrains
Eyes ask questions too…
Like, "What are the things being longed for in you?"

Travelin' like old stones
Carryin' wisdom
But the truths be heavy
Always defined with purpose
Yet still labored, still heavy

Tryin' to overlook this purpose
Tryin' to be brave enough to venture out
Risk being seen
Learnin' to welcome the cascade instead fearing it

Rewetted
Cleanse you, cleanse me

Let us cleanse each other

POETRY REMIX:
*Nayyirah Waheed "Therapy" + Shuntaro Tanikawa "My Sludge"
+ lucille clifton "february 13, 1980" + Me*

*Piled up within me
3,300 minutes of my life you have been
Split you through
In waking time, and in death*

[and Me here, Bleeding Water]

*Keep gathering from all the deaths you & I have died
Tales told, lessons learned and blessings sent
Never needing to regret
That lost color in my eye*

[and Me here, Bleeding Water]

*Discern my own sludge
After being trained to fear the questions, the unknowing
Keep speaking the years from their hiding places
Now even your absence comes of age*

[and Me here, Bleeding Water]

*Things which will never decrease:
Love. Loss. Desire. Pain. Faith. Hope. Discovery. Memory.
Drink all damages into new love
No matter what i say*

*[and Me here, Bleeding Water]
Standing, even when I am falling apart*

Am

I am poetry
Music
& movement
           SPIRITUAL CONNECTION
That seesaw
      of Introvert & Extrovert
I am purpose
I am their dream

Cawfee Talk

The usual -
Sitting in a cafe,
Waiting on Creativity to arrive...
Be it during the morning rush,
Or evening rush hour -
She stays being late.
Lingering on this 24-hour date, that seems like so much time...
But when it comes to her,
It really isn't.

Patience in the slow roast drip,
& Faith sprinkled from the brown sugar packets try to reassure me -
Reminders that the strong and the subtle can co-exist
But ain't no amount of caffeine strong enough to alleviate the doubt
With conscience continuing its compulsion with breakin' nights,
Devouring the rhymes & reasons as to whether this process should
move on

There's a sweetness in the misery tho...
The factual knowingness that she'll never leave me
Just like the honey, caramel, cinnamon and whip cream dispersed in
my cup -
Just because they've dissipated from view,
doesn't mean their taste isn't apparent to the tongue

The GREAT Frenemy, at times -
Comin' and a goin' as she pleases
Lovin' when she comes
Hating to see her leave
Longin' for another chance at it when she appears to be fully gone
from the writing scene
The Extroverted Introvert -
knowin' that a girl like her just sometimes needs to go into hidin'
Enjoying a good spotlight
But only in shared company
Creativity can break-fast,
Stir her footsteps to a quick exit left -
Cuz too much of a good thing can sometimes still be just too much
And I, her loving vessel & confidant, need to learn to accept that

Pondering our last exchange as I grip my pen tight
as if holding it in prayer
I finally see Creativity brimming over my third sip of this latte -
Always making quite the entrance with a subtle sashay and sly grin,
Knowing all along she'd intended on making this date,
But loving to let me simmer in my anxiety & insecurity all the
same...

Creativity leans in, whispering exactly what I need to hear:

Girl, you need to wear me...
Wear me like your favorite see-through dress - drenched in Swarovski
crystals dipped in coconut water and drizzled in white chocolate.
No matter the occasion, I don't deserve to be covered.
I need sun, even in your moonlights.
Our subtlety is innate... Gentle, but permanent.
Caressing your skin, draping over your shoulders...
Planting butterfly kisses on your collarbone...
Tiptoeing my fingertips, making my way down your spine...
I'm always here, even if I seem late.
Late is subjective.
And even when this love affair seems taboo, you know it's a needed
pleasure...
In essence, I seep into you at the same rate in which you sweat me out.
Without a doubt, you are forever mine.
We are a destined pair.
So, believe in me, Love...
Sip slow, savor each rich note...
Knowing I'll forever be paired into your soul.

As gentle as her steps when she first walked in,
I hold her words in my ears
Eternal footprint laid on drums, on memory

Kissing my third eye before she prepares to seemingly leave once more
I unravel my fingers from my pen,
Letting my prayer lift and rise -
Along with the ins and outs of breath in this chest
Along with the bustling patrons coming in & out of this cafe
Along with the steam seeping through this coffee lid -

And hopefully look back at this blank page again.

Not Dead

(Inspired by Ellen Hagan, Blooming Fiascoes)

I am not dead
I am dormant
Like a seed
Seeking sleep and soil and surf and soul
Soaking in Earth energy
Til i can face sunlight with open eyes
Once more
When my time comes to hug Sun's heat
The way she's ever-lovingly embraced all of me

Melodic Juxtaposition: A Poetic Medley

As I sit in the silence of sanctuary, watching air particles float by
I reflect, and embrace the Foundation of My Past –
How I've come from bustling city streets & breezy island roots
I ponder glorified concrete savannahs,
How I nurture its blooming fruit with the same intensity as
the hands that once laid firm upon me

"It gotta be true, If Mama says its so..."
The terrain is prickly,
But simpler for me to traverse now that I've realized my ways

I asked Her a question:
How will I know?
Where do I go?
Who should I be?
Such looming questions be risky; but, I ask anyways
As I dance in this barefoot hip-hop ballet of mine

"My Dear, Read the Stars," Mama says in her grounded reply.
Never interfere with the Stars –
They can't prevent inevitable troubles & heartache,
But rather, Listen closely to their voices –
their voices can freeze negative vibes & melt away devious doubts
simultaneously

Believers, Dream-Keepers –
We Rebel without a Pause
Kaleidoscopic splashes of Love & Light,
We disperse the Vibrancy of Life's Mirror Ball

We Be the "Wordsmiths" – crafting lyrical lesions
Scalpel be my Pen
Paper Be my Body
Incisions of Exactness, Hard & Soft Juxtapose

Flava-full, tangy –
Goodness that originated from the Sun,
Fell through the rainbow that was created from my sunshine,
& from my tears
I taste the words,
Embrace them.
Surprisingly soft in its core
Words intrigue, haunt & linger timelessly
Encasing memories in sugary granules that are clinging to stay whole

Too familiar, but sometimes necessary…
Reality checks me in

Indeed, I Am THAT sharp edge amongst the dull corners
And I haven't any need to apologize for being so

We are Brave, yet still the lamb in the vast meadow –
Gentle
Dreamy
Peaceful,
Brawny
Beastly
& Brave.

So though tomorrow remains the question
I shall replay Mama's straight replies in my mind, and continue to
reflect
Stare – at the wings of this enchanted hair,
Making cures from my roots
Listening to the Stars
Embracing the Subtleties of the Spectacular
Chiseling timeless poetic vibes in stone
Burning my brand in this attempt to blister your flesh
with the passion permeating thru prose

Nothing But the Truth / Spit

Do WHAT
You SAY
& Say
WHAT you
MEAN
Because
IN THE END,
the Only ONE
You're keeping the
TRUTH from
Is YOURSELF

Ambiguous

Horizons in view
Yet, too often
masked in the spews of can'ts, won'ts & impossibles
Making the line skewed
Diagonals -
Seesawing back & forth
Power struggles Continue
to Continue to
Continue
Rather than just accepting the weight's
On both sides
        Percentages and Calculations
        Classification and Categorizations
        Of Tier 1, Tier 2 & Tier 3
            Classic verbiage
        Giving the outward guise of depth -
            When there really isn't any
        Attempting to dig deeper
        Beyond the 45 degree angle
        with a mere chipped looking glass
        When, what is necessary, is a kaleidoscope
        and a scalpel
        Precision
        in instrumenting colorbursts of instructional infinities

Huddled in the masses
But still riding the line -
    Sometimes under the self-serving ring leader's purposeful shadow
    Sometimes self-imposed
Battling between
philosophies & pedagogies
personalities & psychologies

Best Praxis vs. Best Performance
The Academies' War wages on

Don't Sleep

There are no ordinary moments
All experienced serves to teach a lesson

I may appear...
Silent.
Stoic.
Even possibly unaffected.

But, don't be fooled...
Ever pensive, always reflective
Clearly understanding
What
  is
    real
  What
Is
  Not
and, more importantly,
What
I
Deserve

Time waits for no one...
And neither do I.

Resisting Arrest

Always alone
But never lonely - using Her
Cunning & Creativity to
Dash out the devious Devils; stopping them in their tracks as they are
Engrossed by the ENVY of your ways. Attempting to
Find forever in a flimsy moment that, in turn,
Gives way to the
Horrid TRUTH...
Imbecile! Your
JOY shall never come to fruition in pining for the path of another
Kindled passions must be AUTHENTIC
Leaving falsehoods in the past
Moving steadfastly towards the present - be it the actual
NOW, or the
Omnipotent unknown future
Prepare your pathway via
Queries into the SELF
REFLECT
State aloud your
TRUTHS - So What? So Why? Who Be I?
Understand the journey is long, riddled with confusion, blurred
VISIONS and
WISDOMS - some needed. Some actually more wounding.
But, what is necessary will be
eXperienced
YEARNING must be laid to rest. Fill your HEART with
Zeal & zest to CONQUER the Demons & Devils
that aim to arrest your development.

In a Word

Brevity can be poignant
And crossed paths can still affect
future forks in the proverbial road
Stay firm, Feet rooted
in Your Purpose, Your Space
Let the Spirit & the Heart steer
this Journey in
Faith

Oye, Nena...
(Aviso Número Quatro De Mama)

Acuérdate de lo que te decía abuelo -
Los amigos son un peso en el bolsillo y
Las opiniones son como un culo - todo el mundo tiene uno...
Y muchos están lleno de mierda
¿No te ven la magia?
¿Y qué?
You weren't birthed into this light
To worry on what others perceive as your wrongs & rights
Nadie tiene el mapa para vivir tu vida
Esta es la tuya
Y con eso, tienes que hacerlo como te da la gana

Don't Be Like Me, Girl

Don't be like me, Girl
Living in the pangs of past promises unkept
Your heart has been exercised and
EXORCISED for this moment
Chambers built to sustain the remains of memories that deserve
permanent residence
Crafted to run, run, run - JUST like those fresh Nikes you got on
Keep it pushin'!!!
Run those treads – JUST DO IT! ¡Hágalo y ya!

Don't be like me, Girl
Procrastinating...
Waiting on Time to give you the Time to have Time –
Like IF Time will everrrrr really let you touch it?

That body you got be the clock –
Grandfathered in to chime with PURPOSE
Beckoned to toll and tell the story –
My story, OUR Story

Faced to hold the epic journey of the family and continue to carry on
Use those supple, ample arms of yours to Embrace your ticks
EMBRACE Your Ticks...
The tick... tick... tick... as these ferocious feathery fingertips
Dance across this illuminated keyboard –
Yup, I said it – Make it [BIG]...
No [Hank]ies to help them dry their tears, their fears of you
No NEED for You to read their Body Language of Guilt

Shower blank canvases
Trace your lineage across the lines of your composition page and
Across ANY and EVERY platform imaginable!
Make them BE Ready

Don't be like me, Girl
Don't accept their predetermined labels
¡Recuerdate que quien manda aquí eres tú!
So, que te llamen Nuevaaa -
Brand New wit it
Rica wit da sabores Del Bronx y El Borinquen
Invite them sideline hatin' spectators to the Digital Cypher
Let 'em run face first into THIS Magic
Keep Serving up that food to feed the future
Like soil drinking in tears & sweat, and birthing & unearthing gold minds
You are bloomed in Purpose

Don't be like me, Girl
Fearing flight
New Heights in line of sight
Too much
Causing eruptions of assumptions that soon yield
inner consumption of Need to fly

Please ignore the fear of fumbling –
That rumbling??? – It's actually your inner engine
Gearing to propel this work
Hit the tarmac, No turn back
Flying Virgin, but you're learning
No te preocupes… There's always gotta be a first

Don't be like me, Girl
Brimmed
Buttoned up
Thinking that Speaking Up
Will actually yield further disregard

Masking the intended YELL
Into a rather pointed stare instead

Yeah, I feel You –
Those stares serve their purpose

BUT – The SONIC BOOMS required in White Rooms need it all,
Muchachita:
    Mind

       Eyes

          Voice

           Pen

Sharp, Quick. Firm & FELT. Stoic fluidity.
Be that eruption of galactic ash that burns their corneas
BE that Blackhole Sun-Shower

Don't be like me, Girl
Letting Insecurity stand in the threshold of your kitchen
Trying to convince you that this potluck ain't for you

How many times do you need to be reminded to
FEAST ON THIS LIFE!?!
You are anchored
ROOTED – All Tree, No fragile branch
Being nourished from the ancestors' blood, sweat, tears
Y sonrisas, Y movimientos, Y sueños...
Chakras – Opened & Aligned
Wheeling you into your Birthright

Sunlight runs through your veins
Pulsating ripe sweetness – como los plátanos y mangos
de nuestras tierras, nuestras cenas
Grown to be served –
Perfectly sliced & lovingly laid upon the People's plates

We've been waiting far too long to eat.
Serve us, please...

You're really the only one who can.

DEFINITION: Happy

Google's definition: Happiness is an emotional state characterized by feelings of joy, satisfaction, contentment, and fulfillment. While happiness has many different definitions - cheerful, contented, delighted, ecstatic, elated, joyous, pleased - it is often described as involving positive emotions and life satisfaction... Happiness is generally linked to experiencing more positive feelings than negative.
Happy tends to be solely tied to one's work or one's romantic relationships... but...
It is not someone else's job to make me happy.

The elusive happy
Hard to pinpoint
Forever sought out
Forever fought for
Technically defined as:
"an emotional state... involving positive emotions and life satisfaction"

But how long can it last?
How defined can this state be when it inherently is intended to be fluid
In a mental place where "Always" has an expiration date
How can happy be held indefinitely?
Can it ever be?
Or do we only know happy intimately when she has been lost?

As the lead architect in this thing called "Life"
We must build our harmony
Exact precision, with mathematical vision
Of the keys to unlock our happy places
Envisioning multiple states that work to create
A permanent residence to keep happy feeling at home

Próxima Aventura

En mi próxima aventura de vida -
Sea en este mundo o en el cielo
Seguiré llena de dulzura, sin ningunos miedos
Protegiéndome mejor de las amarguras de otros
Que no se la saben vivir bien

Me prometo de ser fiel á mi misma primero
Porque aprendí bien en mi primer turno
Que los corazones de amores cambien como el tiempo
Y yo, también, como reloj antiguo,
No tengo tiempo para parar y quedarme
Sin movimiento

Consuming Rain

I was just here
Staring out my window that overlooks the park...
Sitting in Papi's big, cushy chair.

I thought to myself -
How peaceful it is to let yourself be consumed by the rain.

All the typical city sounds get pushed to the background,
If you really focus your senses on the rain -

How it sounds
How it feels
How it makes everything old & dirty smell fresh & new.

...and even how it tastes -
For the Brave who are willing to take a risk and become one with it.

I feel cleansed and refreshed, yet saddened at the same time.
Just as the rain is hopeful in its suggestion of new beginnings,
it also proclaims a finalization of the past.

Intrigued to see the new start in front of you,
But painful to part ways
Contemplating if they'd stayed
As the past officially says, "Goodbye."

Bittersweet memories along with hopeful reassurances for better
tomorrows and morning afters…

Makes for quite an interesting taste on the palate...
For those willing to take the risk and become one with it

As Simple As

As Simple as −
Awakening to the pitter patter of freshly fallen rain drops on a
window pane
Changing pace as I begin to stir, almost as if trying to sync with my
subtle heart's beat
Apprehension quickly quelled by the hopeful hymns sung by the
choir of birds
on our hood balconies

Birds who despite the climate have never ceased their rehearsal of song

As Simple as -
Gentle nudges on shoulders and soothing whispers in awaiting ears
Letting us know the New Day has come
Be it dreary… Be it sun-filled…
But − at least − it Be
Be ours for the taking, if we learn to listen and allow Her to lead

As Simple as −
Sweet smells of aromatic coffees paving precocious pathways
from the kitchen to the foot of my bed
As if to flirtatiously tickle my toes into waking wiggles just as much as
it tickles my nose to mirror a genie's twitch
With Outstretched arms, Open eyes, Elongated spine −
I Am Woke
Those creaks & cracks in aging bones ring different, mean different
When Being Woke now comes into daily question

As Simple as –
Breathing in deeply
And being able to do it once again
Lungs inhale, Lungs exhale
Diaphragm supporting the ins & the outs
Surging oxygen to everywhere it is thirsted for within this body
Simple acts, yet not so simple
Simple acts once taken for granted now greeted with reverence
And with repeat demand
Simply put: Be Grateful

As Simple as –
The initial crackle from a freshly opened book -
Not necessarily new, but definitely new to these eyes, to these
fingertips -
The sound beckons my learning & expansion,
My contemplation & revelation
Book spine just as mine
Held tightly, uprightly
Prepared to be held,
But patiently waiting for the right reader to behold the tale

As Simple as –
Swooping strokes of pen, or keyboard
Whatever be this day's whim
Gliding upon blank journal pages that have been neglected
far too long
Black & blue inks helping to channel the Blacks & Blues of the Heart
Stops & Starts that yield clearer pictures of what it is I really need
Pages curling upward around my wrist as these lines flow out
Nestled pages being the only hugs I can openly receive right now
But, are embraced nonetheless

As Simple as -
Silence
Encircling, All Encompassing
Surrounding Us,
As it encourages You to love yourself deeply
Absence forced upon us to provoke the Awakening
Closed eyes open wide to the self-care we've been needing
Heeding the Earth Mother's message,
Conceding – Agreeing to disconnect from that which lacks feeling
Being blessed to be able to reacquaint with that
which truly gives life meaning -
Love.

Clock Strikes

Times up
Stroke of midnights no more
No heads up
No ringin' of the alarm
Incomplete items tacked onto this vision board
Become reflections that melt into memories,
Morphing slowly into regret

Time,
Never promised
But always cordially invited
Yearning for more - to see, touch, feel, explore
Not having checked off all these To-Do's, To Wants,
To Haves, To Holds

But, can the Universe just tell me something?

Did the babies I held know that my love was pure?
Did the tears traversed across cheeks know they healed more than
they hurt?
Did mami know that I knew what she really meant when she said,
"Don't be like me"?
Did those broken hearts know that my actions were rooted in my
inner unloving?
Did I purposely thwart happiness for fear of it being taken away?

Answers
I was never meant to know

The Lasts

If I knew that'd be my last cup of tea
Requested of me
Final opportunity to share delicacies
Side-eyes of funnies
And repeated stories of my younger year sillies
Maybe going to chill wouldn't have been the priority

If I knew that that'd be my last laugh
Sitting in la cocina
Soaking in la calentura del horno
Watching novelas and bochinchando
About the way abuela behaved
And the gifts that were gave
And how no matter how much the nietos y nietas had aged
Abuela would still see us niños the same
Maybe heading out into the snow covered street to play in the heaps
Could've waited another day

If I knew that those sneak attack snuggles would be no more
Wouldn't be able to nuzzle on your back as you talked to titi
on the phone
Me waiting patiently for your sole attention once more
To fill you in on my high school daze and
all the crazy I swore just could not wait
To fill you in on my biggest hopes and the greatest escapes I planned
to take
once graduation was conquered,
and life would finally take shape

Maybe I would've talked less and listened more
So the sound of your voice would remain
a permanent resident in this Earthly plane
Living in these longing ears that strain to sustain
Sounds that I can hear no more

If I knew that your storytellin' and soothsayin' had an end
Opportunities to pick your brain on the ways of life
Como how to endure & overcome strife
Helping me figure out the ticks of my clock
Nunca sabiendo que your own corazón was soon to stop

If I knew I wouldn't be able to rely on you forever
That time being precious was more than just something que se dice
Maybe I could've spent less time away
Hiding feelings and mistakes in fear of what you might say
And I'd share all of me with you anyway

If I knew you wouldn't always be readily available
Wouldn't be waitin' for me at our kitchen table
That tu canciones de juventud wouldn't hum through the threshold
To greet me everyday when I came home
Para decirme hello and hug me con las verdades,
Letting me know de las buenas y las malas
Los caprichos y vanidades
To alleviate some of my fears with your tender hands
Fingertips that caressed my face to dry up young love's tears,
foolin' me to think you'd always be here
Maybe I would've stayed in the moment when I had it
Not always try to be so hard, pretending I had it
Todo en control, so systematic
Swearing I was a grown-up when I didn't even know the half of it

If I knew our last kiss would be like this…
Me trying desperately to breathe new life into you
as you spent your entire life doing for me…
Lip Stained purple… so beautifully tragic
As lovely as you always looked in sleep
This was a dream in waking I never wanted to keep
The Iris returning to its slumbered roots
How does one interpret these feelings, a loss impossible to shake loose?

ÓYEME

If I knew this was the last moment I had
That the remainder of my life would be draped
in a lingering cloak of sad
A void that will never fully be filled
Would I have feasted on your love more?
Maybe I could have hugged you harder?
Any other ways to show you that I was proud
to have you as my mother?
Maybe not.

But, I hope the last thing you remembered is how much I loved you.

The Final Act

There's a reality in finality
that is palpable
You hold it
as it holds you
Taste is bitter
The kind that perpetually bites back
Regardless of what you consume
to quelch it
Stuck in space & time
Immovable
Yet surmountable
With the right frame of mind
Difficult nonetheless
But a decision that must be finalized
Just the same

I Was Told

Making the rounds of mandatory pleasantries at my mother's funeral
was never something
I looked forward to, or planned for...
But who ever does, really?
Who ever is actually ready to be at their mother's funeral?

Prior attendances of other family members' final gatherings must
have prepped me well
because I didn't miss a beat as the spotlighted hostess of this
unforeseen January evening

Not a hair out place
Silky straightened perfection unraveled from the doobie I fussed over
in the wee hours the night before
Make-up set to perfection, with the sharpest of wings and
cherriest of lips -
Smudge-proof, of course
Because you don't want to accidentally rub color off on your
guests' cheeks

Outfit sleek and elegant with a just a subtle smidge of flair -
just enough to let em all know who's child I was
Black satin cocktail dress with ruffled knee-length hem traced in red -
cheeried like my lips
Because those lil accents matter, showing purpose and precision of
display

For those mourners who just wanted to be nosey and see what she
looked like in death,
and ask for the details of her parting
I gave them all the grand tour with the unabridged story
Again, and again, and again, and again...
Because it'd be rude not to, right?

Moving with the waves of grief
Greeting everyone as they entered
Making sure they signed the attendance guestbook -
Because heaven help if they didn't.
Making sure everyone received a custom prayer card
with mom's sunrise & sunset -
Because heaven help if they didn't.
Making sure to chat with everyone who was entering the parlor,
recognized or not -
Because heaven help if I didn't appear cordial,
comforting and gracious,
even to semi-recognizable strangers

In between my escorting the mourners to her casket
In between the "I'm sorry's," "My condolences," "She looks so good,"
"You look so beautiful, just like your mother,"
I fell in & out of catatonic states
Dreamin' in the wake
Here in space, but not in body
A tiny unit of energy orbiting in an outer realm of this new "reality"

"She wouldn't have left you now, if she didn't think you were ready..."
The one & only utterance told to me that actually was for me

How I could be standing in a room with so many people
And yet feel SO by myself

Other Side of This

getting back to normal? -
was there ever really a normal to begin with?

embracing a new normal? -
a phrase filled with uncertainty when we can't ever really define what
normal is,
nor should we

the REAL of it -
normal never was, never will be
more of a case of the was & is no more's
the pre- and the post- of it all

but in a world that craves the gratification of clear-cut before & afters
and a focus on those things that are missed
move to challenge Yourself to find and amplify the constants

get out of the Black & Whites
bathe in the Heavenly grays
where cultures, concepts, perceptions, ideas, identities,
memories, lessons, innovations, regeneration and creativity reside

where these constants intertwine with the uncertainties,
making everything inevitably alright
where innervisions come to fruition
proving, again, everything will be alright

pushing through, climbing through,
even damn near crawling through
but, getting through
nonetheless
as is meant, as we are built to do

and in spite of the pains, the aches
arisen like the onset of a newly born day
be that single stem of grass breaking free from deep rooted darkness
from Winter's slumber beneath Earth's surface
subtly peering through that perceived rock bottom to
flirtatiously wink at the Spring Sun

ready and willing to do the work
to blossom into a field of dreams that all my people can grow
their fruit in
a safe space for my blooming, a source of sustenance
for Me & for Us

because I am still here
even when I am grieving
I am still here
even when I am healing
I am still here
even when I am on pause

and regardless of the was and is no more's, the pre- and the post-
my before and afters
I Am Still Here.

still Strong
still Peaceful
still Loved
still Loving
still Bountiful
still Worthy
still Whole
still Magic

on the other side of this

This Is the Year

This is the year -
Self-Love takes the wheel
Hands outstretched
Gripping the 360
Digits clenched intently
It's always been me
Realization of my own self-navigation
Only I can put this into drive

This is the year -
Strapped in
Sights set on the win
Blinders on
Tunnelvision
Everclear
No rearview mirrors allowed
Flooring gas, hauling ass
These bags is packed
Now's the time to reach that next destination
Nuff waitin'
Tired of being patient

This is the year -
That the side hustle becomes main jawn
Poetry morphs into lifeblood rather than a leisurely past time
Straight ta the vein
Got tha masses feenin'
Coursing through ya inner systems
Mapping the pathways of creativity that live within human being
Multiplying
Elevating
Expanding innervision with methodical precision

This is the year -
Similes and metaphors are reunited
Excited
Reignited within the thumps of this lyrical heart
Bumping in ya chest
Like the bass in Tribe track
Flowin hard with da cymbals and the hi-hat
Slappin' on ya eardrums
much disrespect
Ain't no sorrys
Inhale the vibes slow
Take a deep breath
Puff, puff pass to the last stanza left

This is the year -
Pen & pad show out
Red carpet ready
Not apologizing for being late
This flava takes time to incubate
Immaculate connection
Inception wit ya cerebral perceptions
Of what a feminine flow ought to be
Snatchin' up ya mic
Respect, I be Majesty
Yes, Queen Bee done said it
No time for da fake ones, or tha lames

This is the year ya'll gon rememba my name

CHAPTER 3

Jessica Diaz

Urges

Purple majesty
A kiss of love, and of death
Pursed lips pray for both

Foreplay

Veiled in lines, stanzas
Innocence subtly gives way
To sensual gaze

Quiet, Masterful
Scrutinized from tip-to-toe
Inquisitive eyes

Hide, and come get it
Catch her if you think you can
Stamina is key

Poured from Life's pitcher
A refreshing trickle in
Your cupped, eager hands

Oye Nena...
(Como lo dice Abuela)

Esas caderas fueron hechas en candela
Quemándole los ojos a todos
Dios le guarde las manos
A esos que traten tocartelas
Sin amor y aprecio

For the Record

This luvin' be like da old skool
Put tha needle on da record
Raspy, grizzly, smooth
Only play that puts me in tha groove
Scratch tha surface
Tha mo' scratches, tha betta
Let's me know this luv is vintage
Sleek, black, stroking
Reverberating
Makin' hearts skip tha beats
Buttery smooth -
Like jazz
Like cognac
Take a pull in
And swallow the bass line slow
Feel it as it feels you
Rotate me while cupping that spindle
Ridin' tha grittiness of it all
Play wit me on my B-side
Classics always play on repeat
Flippin' scripts
Til tha playa overheats

RIPE

Presented on a platter
Ripe, golden
Glistening
Piled high
Stacked
Hands grasping each side
Hip-to-Hip
Parting me gently
Opening up to see the core
Sweet, juicy, moist
Fruit-bearing center
Epitome of existence
Carved out perfectly
She waits tenderly
Ready to bear the future

Heart Speak

Enduring presence
Truth never needs to yell
She murmurs messages
Callings
The yearnings
Rooted in bone
Flow in blood
Seep out of skin
I get lost too often in the external
Consumed by the bravado of the white noise
Catch myself I must
Because these distractions, abstractions
Only serve to produce chain reactions of complacency,
Malignant stagnancy
These are often the fears disconnecting us
Me & my Heart Speak
She knows this
Can't lose the pulse that binds us
But, again, truths have no need to yell
Subtlety in volume doesn't make the whispers less true
Heart makes sure to remind me that
Dichotomy is my being
No need for apologies for multifacetedness
There need be no apologies for choosing You first

So talk On to me
Talk In to me
Speak over me, gentle Heart
Soft-spoken twin
Soaked in electric sugar
Seldom seen, rarely tasted in the raw
But still in clearview
Still tickling the pensive, patient tongue
Quite content in speaking before being spoken to
When the feelings become ideas, and hopes become plotlines
Bottled energy becomes vocal action
As the stuff of heart struggles to stay at the brim
Both vessel and chamber
Cupping my essence
Safeguarding my gentle
Stay true, Heart
Keep me honest
I'll quiet down long enough to listen
I promise

"Love Requited: A Prologue"

Etched in Her Mind's Core
Linger memories of He
Vivid as Daybreak outside of Morning's Window

As persistent and "hope-full" as the dawning of a New Day
She welcomes His presence - Even when He isn't physically here

Internalizing His breath
Taking Him in
Embracing Him fully -
Fusing flesh & essences with each moment they've spent

Wrapping Him up tight, Holding Him close –
Be it with Her arms, or Her legs
She feels the gravitational pull of their orbits

Cascades of stars trickle down
Droplets dripping from their fingertips
As caresses are gently laid

Looking at their intertwined hands,
Realizing that it is possible to scoop a bit of Heavenly Galaxy
With feet still being firmly planted within the Earth Mother

Rooted in Soil's realism
Yet unafraid to reach for helpings of stardust
From the system's Milky Way

Both feed Their Souls —
Understanding that they evolve from
Everything & Nothing all at once
Requiring the bluntness of Earthly existence,
And the whimsy & mystery of the Universe —
The kind only Thinkers & Dream-Keepers such as themselves can see

He sees Me
Simultaneously sharing He
Cautiously embracing newfound faith in celestial feelings
Engulfed within the electromagnetic impulses
that dance between their frames
All this - When Sir Mars decides to
venture once more towards His Lady Venus
Much obliged, He's welcomed In

Venusian-Martian Dichotomy / "So We Meet Again..."

Lady Venus: Hot & Hellish, yet bringer of the Light
Like Lucifer before the fall - Heavy
Her seemingly smooth plains having been marred by volcanoes' past
This Lady is in constant flux – Building Herself, Breaking apart
To build Herself once more
Her exact composition forever a mystery
But, the vibrancy of Her zebra-like stripes continue to lure Him in...

Sir Mars: Iron-clad core - Striking in His reds, oranges and golds
Twice as bright as the brightest Star, Yet subtle...
But, trust me, He's easily seen
Warmer in the past, thirds of His heart appear dark
He's uncertain – Not of Himself... Not of Her...
But, of the risk worth taking
So he obscures His surface within His memory storms

Mars knows Her well, yet not at all
He gazes upon Her, yearning to speak what he's waited eons to say
But, instead, only choosing to speak through His orbital waves

Venus accepts that
Lady's learned to read beyond mere lips, tongues and words
a long time ago
She allows Him to stare - Carefully revealing Her secret codes
in the process
Mars, filled with grooves...Venus loves to tune into His channels

84 steps seemingly in the right direction
159 more to go to circumvent Her axis
Slower than Her Earthly sisters – Always purposely making certain
to rotate in their opposite direction
... And that is okay with Him.
Always taking His time too,
She respects the 24 hours and 40 minutes to His days
But, never be fooled - Just because the magnetism arrives gentle
Doesn't negate the fact that it exists

Smooth on some sides, Rugged on others
Lady summons her waters to caress and carve into His innermost parts
Filled with Earthly minerals, with twinges of evergreens –
Proof of where He's originated
Proof of His connectivity to the Earth Mother
Proof of His ability to Live, and give Life

Sweetening Her (r)evolutions like saccharine
Love flickers from golden-brown butterscotch tongue
Breathing reimagined Life through the obstacles that had once
overwhelmed Her amethyst heart
He oxides Her, Becoming her air

Their dance is eternally sacred
At times, somewhat shy – Each asking the other 1st for permission to
come across their cosmic boundary
Lightyears living within inches of each other –
- Flowing in the same circle
- Courting identical waves
- Listening in on the same ciphers
- Tasting similar highs & lows, though in different dimensions of time
They see each other clearly now – within this cosmic tease

Crafting cyclones, causing rises and falls within His chest
Mars continues to contemplate Her – Questioning Himself even more
How could she possibly be both His Evening & Morning Star?
Surfacing yellowish-whites, Harboring crimson within
All while wearing su corona brillante
que parece como suspirar sobre su rostro

Can she ever understand how Mars sees Her?
This being exactly It – the It constantly alluded to,
seldom seen in this vastness of existence
The absorbing and reflecting of energies –
simultaneously, purposefully... Destined to be
Fully conscious of the Newness;
but, realizing that Newness only lasts about a week
Theirs is a love that was, and has always, been meant –
Weathering solar flares & supernovas in reaching this place

Sir loves His Lady for being the epitome of dichotomy –
Earth's spit-fire fraternal sister
Rooted, yet ethereal –
With Her smooth plains marred by vitriol,
More than blood & water - There's lava coursing these veins

Nevertheless, He's learning to embrace My Lady with empathy –
Acknowledging that He is Being of the same dichotomy himself
The more Sir Mars realizes of Himself, the more He allows Lady to see

The most passionate of combinations
Beyond seeing each other – They see within each other
Vibrations oscillating to and fro
Continuously completing & repeating this energy circle

Finally admitting that questions & doubts aren't necessary when
Galaxies collide
You simply just: Let. It. Be.

Happy Neptune

Shy away from Sun's limelight
2.8-ish billion miles traveled to that self-proclaimed own
island of happy
Full
In & of itself
This god of atmospheric sea
And celestial shimmer
Bodies drawn to his possibility

Can you inhabit me?

His cool, blue stare never answers
But that subtly sexy glimpse of a smirk
Gives me a definite maybe

Cursive Q's

Quiet
Very underused
Very underaccessed
Very underestimated
Seldomly addressed by their first name
Quintessential underdog
Yet quite the regal fellow
A quagmire of sorts...
Quasi invisible. Until he opens his mouth...

Dapper, man-
Be it with his top hat
or the sashay of his quaint tails
Put together like a quilt
stitched with tethered ropes and faint traces of the finest silks
His existence is a quadratic equation
Made whole from all the variables that are pieced together
And though his exes appear to be unknown,
The impression left behind definitely encourages some answers

Surprisingly quenching the thirst for novelty
when he appears in the queue
Dropping witty quips to rouse the crowd's attention
Quizzical stares are the regularity as we wonder, "Who is he?
... And why hadn't we met before?"
Questions of their origins still abound
But, he continues to create quakes of curiosity
within every syllable spoken

No singular quote could ever capture their unique savvy
No dainty quill substantially equipped to ink the tale of this legacy
No possibility to lessen the quickening of my fragile heart's beating
The quarrel ensues - with conscience and common sense
trying to steer me away from the charming quirks of this gent
Reminding me of the qualifications I'd sworn to demand
for her safety
Heart & mind quibble incessantly

I resent my attraction
Yet, I admire him all the same
Whether adolescent & naive, or fully matured & wise,
The theatrics of their curves continue to erupt in intrigue,
That simultaneously almost appear to quell
the unknown flames of desire
Lying reluctantly dormant within this queen

Ocean waves of brilliance cascade from each swirl made
with each word that rolls off his tongue
My face reading of how hard it is to actually persuade my ears to
quit listening
To his poetry
To his jests
To his song

Was I meant to just be a part of the quota?
Or is this admiration a quantum physics lesson in destiny?

Dreamkeeper

His mind run on She
Creeping into dream
States in Waking, Static Clings

Prototypes

They do exist
I know that everything comes in cycles
And close knock-offs are the name of the game
But a replica will never be
The Original
And those recycled lovers of yours
Will never be
Me

Cold-Hearted?

This heart ain't dead
Far from it
My love just gets sleepy
Lies dormant
Needing slumber to regenerate
Be ready for potential orbiting
Only seeking love that leads to new heights
Outer limits, or I ain't wit it

Blame it on the Global warming
Because my heart can't distinguish what it feels
Too many temperature changes in the fingertips
Of those I trusted to caress my heart

Jessica Diaz

Flake

FROSTED - masked with your sugary sweet disguise...
Or, PLAIN - seemingly just ohhh sooo real
Straight Out Tha Box - supposedly true to what your explicit
outer packaging states
Or, Swimming in a Bowl of Milk - drowning in a sea of insecurities
& bullsh*t from your past

You may TASTE good, LOOK good...
Filled with a nice, hearty CRUNCH at 1st bite!
BUT, when I check your boxtop expiration date,
I realize you are totally STALE

...At the end of the day, even more than a flake,
You're just plain ol' CORNY

GET OUT of my damn cupboards, F*CKIN' FLAKES!

...I was never much of a cereal person anyways.

*Dedicated to all those REAL WOMEN who have - or are in the
process of - clearing out their stores' shelves to make room for some
FRESH & ORGANIC produce. No longer settling for pre-packaged,
overly-processed JUNK FOOD. Enjoy, Ladies! Bon appetit!

No Maybes

Forever, love lost
Was never found to begin
With an either / or

The Call

I waited for your call
Eager to answer
But what I heard was silence

Dead silence

Why generate anticipation
to devastate with goodbyes -
Lingering pain, withstanding time

Farewells, always the heavy & hard kind
Like the barrier being rebuilt around this heart
As I question why I even bothered to let this romance start

REGRET

Indecipherable
But it's supposed to be
Heart palpitations STILL
when you're next to me
Trying to run but
Ya feet must be on backwards tho
Cuz you always return to facing me
Place to be
In between these knees
I dunno know who's getting off more when you're pleasing me
Teasing me
Admitting that you stay missing me
Nicknamed me "Waldo" cuz you stay searching for me
Yearning for me
Staring hard
Scouring
In the crowd looking for me
Never realizing how right I was in being
When I'd say there was only one me
Should've believed me
No need to lie, especially to the one where my heart be
Mix the salty and the sweet
Laffy taffy memories of what our life together used to be

Coulda be
Knowing you royally fucked up
Now you trying to get back to your destiny
Mind running on She
Sound sensibility was lacking in your brain chemistry
Ever thinking you'd find more than the best of me?
Cherry lips poppin'
Curves bangin', Body Wonderland an'
paired with the matching intellectuals
Droppin' knowledge, Intelligence dispensary
Eye conversations sharing world histories
Insane sexual chemistry
Catching flights to arrive at even deeper feelings
Diving willingly into my ocean of milk & honey
Loving life, and growing within it
Thick and thin of it
I was totally in it -
Back then

Indecipherable
Not comprehending
This ending
of the lovestrings being plucked
Heart getting unstuck
How am I not waiting anymore?
No three's company
No need to knock on my door
Fuck living in a daydream
It's over now
Crystal in this intuition
This woman's work is only to soar to new heights
Tunnelvision
Clear with precision
Gotchu feelin' shaken & stirred
How can I no longer be stressin' if you textin'?
Easy, because my life encompasses a happy beyond our we
I found a peace in me

That is more profound,
Mattering more than if I happen to have your piece in me
Satisfying my own libido
Oops, oh my
I can't help it, pulling a Tweet on me
Your turn to accept that your presence
Ain't worthy of my periphery
Commitment to my contentment is my only necessity
Acknowledge my inherent multiplicity
I just need all the woman in me
Thriving In the suburbs of joy
At the intersection of independence and excellence
Effervescent,
Even shockin' myself with how fly I be
How far I can see
My life going without the burden of you secretly hatin' on me
Gots no worries in relation to you, or any Prince Charmings
The luxury of time lies confidently in my broken clock
Not societally stapled to anyone's nuclear thoughts
I'm birthing the next generation every time I talk
Birthing seeds every time I scribe my thoughts
So much more amazing than you thought -
Back then

Oye Nena...
(Otro Dicho De Abuela)

Las flores necesitan agua
pero sol tambien
So cuando el te pone los ojos encima
Dile que lo haga con mucho calor
Esos ojos se pueden sentir si el amor es puro

Te lo prometo, nena
Te lo juro

Fortune Cookie

Laying upon his palm
Caved in upon herself
Encasing her secret
- Bashful to share it; but eager to let it be known as well
Only a corner of the prophetic scroll can peek out to tempt
her readers
Waving amorous red text, floating across ethereal ocean-white
sea foam
Reaching out delicately like blooming flower buds peering out
To greet Spring's subtle, but sustainable rains

She lay in the palm of his hand
Caved in upon herself
As he holds her, asking – What is this message? Am I ready to know?
Will he lick her sweetness, soften her coating
Opening her gently, to reveal the wisdom and wonders she'd carried
in her core for him these lifetimes?
Or, be abrupt.
Impatient.

Tight grip upon her curvature, Crumblin' her façade in his haste
to get to where he selfishly needs to go – Disregarding her thoughts
once more as to how they should journey there
In his impatience, he closes his fists
Manly hands –
Soft on her arches. But, destructive
to the tale she believed she destined to tell

She lay in the palm of his hand
Crumbled upon herself
Cracked – A mosaic of sugar crystals and youth-filled whimsy
Fully exposed, no shell to hide within
The message revealed, finally.
In plain sight.

Confucius says: Fragility is strength running the risk of being broken.
Being broken will always reveal learning – Be it of Love & Loss
Be it of Need or Want
Be it of Yes or Know
And,
Certain she is – Now
As she lay in the palm of his hand
Caved in upon herself
She finds strength in knowing that she can regenerate
Wholeheartedly, once again

The Now

Live in the moment
Eyes wide shut, trusting the fall
Will revive your heart

Body Language

My eyes tell my lips how to move across your face
Trace your forehead with the gentlest of grace
Parted ever so with hummed breath
As we coordinate to plant kisses as blessings upon your stressed brow
Eye sees the creases love lost has made
Eye sees the lonely that has settled in the lines
And even though I'm so scared to touch you sometimes
because I don't know if you're ready to feel me,
If you'll trust the sympathy that brims upon this tearful lash line
My lips still wait patiently
Watching your feelings and butterfly kissing each one

Chemistry Applications

Dating App #1: "Plenty of Fish"
More so – "Pond of Falsehoods"...
Trying to remain hope-full in this sea of barracuda
Still pulling a Dory, swimming steadfastly despite Her tattered fins
and partially sloughed off scales
She believes in Rejuvenation / RE – In – car – Nation
So though some of these specimen be tainted flesh
She believes that the fresh waters in which they were both birthed
and continue to co-exist,
Do have the power to cleanse the superficial psyche
Returning them to the origins of purity,
To the Innocence of Love's original intent
But, only when these willful barracuda decide it to be so.

Oscillating between wading in the shallow end – engaging in
pompous pleasantries and
Deep-Sea Diving alone for roughly 40 miles,
Pushing feverishly against the currents to get to "The Good Ones" –
Rather than settle for the muck at the surface
Excavating – extremely exhausting
This spelunking in water-filled caves
- Dodging the nets of the thirsty
- Brushing off "The Leftovers"
- Shucking oyster after oyster in search of a pearl...

Yes!... A Cultured pearl:
Large in His Heart's size
Warm in His luster
Balanced in His Hardness
Wild in His Rarity
Colorful in His Aura
– in His Pinks, Whites, Creams, Champagnes
- His Blues & Blacks, Blacks & Blues
Where, Oh Where is this elusive pearl hiding?

Dating App #2: "OK Cupid"
More so – "OK, Tragic Comedy"
Once again, ironically, Cupid's bow has seemingly struck –
as in the past
But, to Whom & by Whom is the real Uncertainty
Pensive over the "Whys & Why Nots",
She must consider the true question:
*To Be or Not to Be –
Authentic, Audacious and Alluring with the Classy; but not the assy
*To Be or Not to Be –
Headstrong, Harmonious, and Inherently Happy as a "Table for 1"
– Wanting you, but not Needing you
*To Be or Not to Be –
Focused, Forward-Thinking, Free-Flowing Energy –
Explosive in brilliance in Her own singular right
*To Be or Not to Be –
Independent, Intrinsic & Intelligible –
Without fear that My "Me" won't intimidate Your "You"

But, alas, though these queries can never fully be answered, She
holds securely to the Shakespearean motto: "All's well that ends well"

Her Love is strong;
But not meant to be stronger for the unlovable
She lies in this Realism –
Carefully removing the cynics & embracing the inevitable laughter
that comes with hindsight
Believing firmly that: "What is meant to Be, will Be"

Dating App #3: "E-Harmony"
More so – "Ayyyyyye Dios mio!"

Understand that computer-generated algorithms and
laundry lists of questions
upon questions
upon questions
upon questions
Cannot dictate the court-ordered rulings of the Heart

It may seem like a "Match.com" through the fiber optics
of the computer screen
But, you won't be rumbling with this bee
unless you comin' with the right amount of bumble –
Be humble –
Know that She is aiming to connect with your emotional depth 1st!

May have Tindered – Right-swiped rather than Left
But, don't let that lead to suggestions of bending Her,
or pouring your coffee on Her after just meeting
No amount of "Likes", "Swipes" or coffee beans i s
going to tell Her heart when to feel the Elusive "It"

No, no... not "IT", Sir. Smh.
The proverbial "It" –
The chemistry,
That 60 / 40 split of organic love & undeniable compatibility
That "It" that permeates the skin even before He has gotten
the nerve, or cue, to touch it

Don't be afraid...
May seem like a daunting task,
But anything worth having requires hard work, correct?

So, Dear Sir –
I will go home alone. Kiss your cheek as I bid you a fair goodnight...
And, know that if This is meant to be "It", you should be fantasizing
about my energy rhythms,
instead of *just* my body tonight

Resuscitate

Water glistens across these calloused fingertips
Baptizing hurt & worries,
Resurrecting hope and those somethings to look forward to
Clasped, cupped
Water, like hope
Hard to hold onto
But to try try again is a must
Such as with water, without hope there would be no life at all
Elastic heart, prolonging this life
Ensuring that these heart wells never run dry
That the dampness held within its chambers
Refuses to diminish the residue of hope left behind
Savage subtlety
Waters ability to connect us
Wake us
Beckon us to transfer, evolve
Not always having to be hard
Able to carry on in spite of the uncertainty
Of how many beats remain
Slough off the icy shavings surrounding this heart
Water ripples mimicking heart's beat
As she emerges anew
calling out into forever for another chance
Affirmation that once had, not forgotten
Let these waters lessen the burdens of a loveless body gone cold
Postpone the fatigues of this weary soul
Rehydrate, Returning love to its fluid state
Moisten these hope-filled lips as I sip you slow
As I let love's waters flow once more
Greeting the potential to boil with anticipation of bliss
Crystalline, yet forever stained
In his kiss

Lost City

Let's escape to a Lost City
Hidden from distraction
and others' jealousies
From societal timetables and expectations
Away from the scrutinies of what they make Love out to be
We can travel the road less taken
Doesn't matter if there are no markers to tell us where to go
Because where it exists
is where we choose to go
Is where we wind up undoubtedly
Together

Let's find our Lost City
Lost, but not in reckless abandon
Rather lost in sacred assurance
That in this Love is where we both want to be
Our sacred space -
Frozen solid in certainty rather than in fear
where time only ticks forward if we decide to stop kissing
Where the only decision that ever needs to be made is
How I want to hold you, or where you want your caresses to be laid
Where distinction between hand and thigh,
fingers and lips isn't possible
Because we can't bear to not touch each other
Tracing pathways with tip & tongue to discover
the hidden treasures of deep love
As if this map to forever could have ever been crafted
if it wasn't for the discovery of us

ÓYEME

This Lost Place
Seems no one knows where to find it,
Or have just given up the search
Where love is only impacted
By the you & the me involved
The moves we make synergistically
In tandem, In compliment
In communion, In commitment
To this partnered love journey
Destined in fate,
But nurtured on purpose

Such a blessing to wander in this life with you
Such a blessing to know that you & me are not lost at all
Rather, found in Love -
Within ourselves, and with each other
Where my city stands in the safety of your heart
Where you heart is my home

Linger

Windswept reveries
Cascading on borrowed time
As sunshine peeks out

Raindrops masking pain
mirages , deflecting shame
Humbled, I sustain

Milky Way cascade
Visible, yet seldom seen
Supernova waves

Dreamer in waking
Unapologetically
Fairy-dusted Soul

Whimsy overflows
Kaleidoscopic Love Bursts
Raging Subtleties

Artsy, Poetic
Rebellious Freedom-Seeker
I need to ignite

Breezy like the day
Fire lingers in my mane
Hope-Full in my gaze

And on this page

SHE IS _____.

SHE IS Fresh Flowers -
Beauty visible, though Subjective
Comprised of many colors, Her energy changes –
With seasons,
With moods,
And with surroundings – Both physical & social

Petals plucked, pulled from Her core on wasted wishes of the past
Slowly, but surely, She regenerates
Bold, supple, unique – Better than before

Constantly seeking renewal, rebirth…
And though She's experienced Death many, many times,
She still manages to continue to blossom – Again, and again,
and again.

SHE IS Earth –
Filled with hidden wonders that She hasn't even discovered yet...
Visible canvas shows all sides of Human Existence –
The Beautiful,
The Magnetic/Kinetic Forces,
The Purposeful Magic & Mysticism of Earthly Creation:
Conception, Birth, Life & Living, Death & Dying,
and Conception once more
Feeling the weight of Others upon Her earthy surface,
She remains Light –
Using Gravitational pulls
to redirect those channels that aim to hurt Her...
Instead, drawing nearer those Heavenly Bodies that wish
To exchange rejuvenating Energies with Her

Constant is the rotation of this axis
Stopping is not a possibility
Because this spin impacts many others – more than some may think
And, the further She evolves, the further We Revolve

SHE IS Sea –
EVERYWHERE.
Endless, Energetic – Potential & Kinetic.
Enduring. Ever-changing. Ever-necessary.

Surely crucial to existence, no?
For if it were not the case,
then She wouldn't have been summoned to be Here...

To cascade over rough edges,
To slough off dead matter – Revealing deeper underlying freshness...
To expand...
Reaching vast corners – many not dared to be touched
To seep in...
Wearing down seemingly impenetrable facades with unyielding
patience & consistency

Mighty enough to pull you in,
Cleanse you in Her tidal waves,
Baptize you in Her salty wetness –
And, ironically, make you thirst for more...

But, do know, She is just as able to wash you away
into bottomless depths
If one chooses to break the covalent bonds that bind Her core
Latent forces, but massive nonetheless

SHE IS Sun –
CONTINUOUS.
Pondered and Talked about – in Her phases of darkness & light
Center of Everything by Creation's will
Life - She creates it, makes it, takes it away
All in a matter of a day

Forces attempt to burn this fire out
This blaze is beyond extinction
Comprised of several passions - When one flare dies down,
another is summoned forth

Giving you warmth when it's needed
Playing peek-a-boo behind cumulus cloud cover
when She needs to remind you of
How much She is loved
Slowly rising up from horizon lines each morning to nurture you
Planting sun-drenched kisses upon your eyelids
And Sensually laying down at dusk,
letting you trace Her settling shadows with your gaze

SHE IS Woman –
Juxtapositions & Contradictions
Delicate, daring, daunting intelligence
Fierce, flowy, feline strength
Sweet, subtle, sexual prowess
Knowing She can, but not having to brag to prove a point
That appealing glow let's you know the magic that lies within Her
and Her walls

Toiling long and hard, but always guaranteeing a win
Investing time and energy excavated from a seemingly bottomless pit
Doing what needs to be done, when it needs to be done -
Knowing it is Her charge to do so...
Knowing no difference in chromosome can dictate
what she can and cannot do

Birthing future Queens & Kings...
Raising libidinal temperatures to extremes...
Arousing senses with a singular stare...
Evoking calls to action simply because She can...
And awakening your curiosity & intrigue
with the mere stroke of Her pen...

SHE IS all of these things –
Filled with Nouns and Verbs
An ally in this fight for Oneness
Just asking to be nurtured in return
See HER in Her pieces, and as a whole
And She will listen to your whispers upon Her ears
Willing to grasp your hand in taking this journey
While knowing She is strong enough to walk it on Her own

Heart Guard

I am *Love*.
From hair root to tippy toe,
It ebbs & flows throughout this being.
Somewhat temperamental -
Curious to gauge how my changing states will feel
upon another's skin.
Sometimes firm - like waves unabashedly caressing shore's line
in the light of day.
Sometimes light. Almost feathery. *Fun* & flirtatious - like the bee
sensually teasing its flower, unsure if it be ready to take a bite.
I make sure to *penetrate* first, because it's a lot easier to infect
the lovelorn heart of another than risk having my own vessel
overwhelmed...
Because as *passionate* as I am, I am fiercely *devoted* to protecting
my own heart.

Adrift / Afloat

Words and writings seem to flow so effortlessly between the two -
Similar to the way that waves do

His current continues to pull her in
Something beyond control
Powered by the eternal, Mother Moon

Not the novice swimmer,
But she realizes the difference in this buoyancy
Floating in his ocean,
Levitated softly
Yet, simultaneously,
Held strong

Connected -
Comparable to the interlocking of lover's fingers
To the synergistic rise & fall of breathless chests
To the sunset, as she lays down with horizon
Gifting a long kiss goodnight

Fear as well as anticipation abound
No land in sight
She's only encapsulated by 1000's of stars -
Each of which this ocean heart has wished upon for so long

ADJUST

Quite the adjustment
Learning to hold you
Only in my heart,
not in my hands
and within these eyes

X, WhY?

X marks the spot
Where I left my heart
Fighting so hard to escape the past
Thinking it's just a matter of how to run
Steadily fast

Inadvertently, Unconsciously
Yet actually, moving towards it
Alas, clinging to the past even tighter
Clasped in the grip
Choked
Suffocating Present in the aftermath

Should my heart be concerned?
Does not everything come back in cycles?

But, I'm gently reminded that a replica will never be the original
Nor will my heart ever beat quite the same again

Y
Because it was never meant to
Especially after experiencing the love of You

Phonetic Phrenetic

The Coulda Woulda Shouldas
The Have & Have Nots
The Forgives and / or Forgets
The "What I meant to say was..."
Or the "It's not you, it's Me..."
And the oh so infamous,
"I love you, but I'm not In Love with you..."

What it all boils down to is this:
What are you really trying to tell me?

Sounds like...
You coulda paid more attention but were simply unaware
You woulda spent more time if you had it to spare
You shoulda listened to the warning signs, yet you didn't.
So deal with it, I'm over it
I'm out of this

Sounds like...
You have it all, inside your proverbial bubble
You have the world at your feet - according to Facebook
You supposedly have everything figured out - just like Wikipedia
But, I haven't got the time to waste
Haven't got the patience to wait
Haven't got the heart to break it to you that
You're totally played

Sounds like...
You expect forgiveness
Assume it should be so easily remitted
An earned right simply because an apology was given

Forget your infidelities?
Forget your disloyalty?
Forget your misleading words?

That I cannot.

Presenting foiled boxes of chocolates
With syrupy sappy postcards after the fact
Might as well be serving up a platter of sh*t
Spitting hot garbage
Tongue splintered
Razor bladed with freshly sheared tips

Forgive, I won't
Forget - an impossibility
All I can guarantee is a lesson learned and a new perception
A clearer view set forth before me

Sounds like...
You meant to be truthful
After you were caught
You meant to say your feelings had changed,
Right after you locked in the "next best thing"
You meant to be only a friend,
But sex happened to get in the way

No worries
Cuz I meant to say that I never needed you or it anyways
Takes much more than a young handsome face and
An hour long lay
To keep a pretty kitty like me entertained

Sounds like...
You think I'm awesome
Perfection
Woman of your dreams -
Is that so????
Be that the case, I'd hate to see how you treat the
Woman of your nightmares
Pretty-pleases and "Oh, I dunno"
"I just wasn't ready." back then.
What makes you think you are now?

The only two things we can agree on are that:
    1) I am pretty f*cking awesome!... and
    2) Like diamonds, I shine bright and cut like glass.
Slicing raw, to the core
Reflecting back at you what you deemed to be hidden flaws

The love you saw as a possibility in others
Was way too much of a reality in facing me
Other shes were potential
My love's been kinetic -
Too frenzied
Too Intense
Too Tangible
Too Real

The attributes you claim to seek -
Strength
Smarts
Independence
Creativity
Were actually the characteristics you fear most

Can't handle greatness placed in your pathways
Faced with internal shortcomings
Your lackluster
Tryna blame me for your insecurity
That's what this all sounds like to me

The Coulda Woulda Shouldas
The Have & Have Nots
The Forgives and / or Forgets
The "What I meant to say was..."
Or the "It's not you, it's Me..."
And the oh so infamous,
"I love you, but I'm not In Love with you..."

What it all boils down to is this:
I've always been too much for you to handle
Understandable.
This aura holds much weight
Go get less
Low hanging fruit, much more your speed
There will be no more tears shed
No more accusations or pleas
Let bygones be bygones

Sounds like that's the cue to leave

Afraid Of

Afraid of admitting the truth
Afraid of asking for it in return
Afraid of hearing the words spoken -
Words weighing heavy with the possibility of hurt

I'm afraid of falling...
Afraid that I already did
When I promised myself so, so hard that
I wouldn't do this again

Afraid of seeing clearly
That he's not the one for me
But even evermore afraid of forever being alone again

Afraid of him and that allure
That pulls me in
Afraid that I won't be able to resist
Ever wanting to see him again

What's worse -
Admitting the fear
Or letting yourself behold this gift?
So obvious how we feel
Eyes without choice but to mirror it
Is it still considered a secret if we purposely try to flee from this?

I can admit that I am afraid
When do you plan on doing the same?
Will you ever?
Your admission could be the reason I stay
But, if you can't, then I'll be left with no choice
I'm afraid that I will have to leave.

Love

Like the hue of freshly blooming irises
Similar to the deep red in a sparkling glass of merlot
Aubergine, just as a sweet saccharin-filled plum
Love
As a lipstick stain lingers on the rim of a wine glass
Or as the gentle reverberating echo that replays in one's ear
when hearing love professed for the very first time
Love
How can something so warm, seeming permanent & consistent
In its beauty & existence
Actually be so fragile & fleeting?
Love

Listen

You know how they say that when you're purchasing a car,
the right one that you're
meant to get will speak to you? -
It'll tell you if it's a lemon,
A diamond in the rough,
Or in mint condition.
Well, you know what I finally realized?
Men speak too.
Sometimes via audible words
At times through body language
And, in most circumstances, by what they do (or don't do)
So rather than kick a hubcap and cry and yell
for the umpteenth time,
"I didn't see this coming!"
Next time, I'll just listen.

Crashing Into Reality

This love is like a fucking car crash
A head-on collision with me as the designated driver -
Full-throttle
No brakes
Though I'm totally unintoxicated, I might as well be
Because I see the oncoming catastrophe and I still am
revving my engine
Pumping on the gas -
Hard
Everything inside of me is screaming for me to stop!
But, instead, I unfasten my seat belt, slam on the gas and
run through the red light
Catapulted through the air
Ejected / Rejected
Arriving at a grinding halt

Why didn't I notice those hazard lights being on?
Driving on the freeway doesn't mean we are ready to let go of the wheel

Counterfeit

Seemingly 100% authentic
Just like an original
Believable
The prototype of what Truth embodied would be

I am abruptly reminded that there is
No such thing -
No certification of authenticity
No copyright
No originality
WHAT-SO-EVER

> A replica of the same ol' same
> No depth
> No value
> All surface
> Superficial

As worthless as a penny with a hole in it
Imposter,
Take off the mask
Reveal true self
Or run the risk of being a fake "buck" being passed from
Soiled hand to soiled hand
until, eventually, placed out of circulation

A single, torn, withered bill
One who has lost their inner value
Because the preference was to seem worthy by way of artificialities -
False appearances
False words
False perceptions,
Of you & of me

You're counterfeit
The one thing that can surely be believed

Unbreakable

Resilient, be brave
Battered, bruised; but not broken
Spirits stay holy

Soul's Eye

There is a booming voice
Ruminating in my silence
Please don't perceive my lack of audible response as
a sign of disregard -
It is rather a designation of great care

Choosing not to speak just to fill surrounding space
With scattered waves
Preference is to act as the pebble
One leap is all it takes for my ripples to abound
Uninhibited by expansive distance
The magnitude of this heart is powerful
More so in what hasn't been said versus what has

Don't see it as fear
Not intimidation
No need for waiting to speak until spoken to
No stuttering as a plan on how to birth a believable lie

The lack of words stems from the stammering beat
Of a scarred, fragile heart
That is holding on to its last hope that
This one will be it

Flashback the fears
Reignited, flaming sores
With false retellings of forever afters
Again, I make no sound
No words
No replies
No waves
Withholding the ripple

Please don't perceive a lack of audible response
As a sign of disregard -
Rather as a designation of great care
Because I refuse to say those 3 little words
Create a false start
When I suspect that you can't go the distance

So, yes, mums the word
Tongue-tied,
For now

There is a booming voice
Ruminating in my silence
Immeasurable through decibels
Only through the depth of
this Soul's Eye

Sunday Tea & Sympathy

Can I be your cup of tea?
Listen to the recollections with a sympathetic ear
Filling, and needing to be filled

Hoping to support the purge
Pour into these caressing walls with subtle simmers
Love that evaporates and condenses simultaneously
Glistening on porcelain curves
Aromatic essences pooling in the arches
Chiseled.
Sitting pretty –
Tall, perched and waiting to be cradled in thirsty hands
Yearning hands
Nurturing hands
These hands
Hands that hold close
Healing & tasting the gentle exhale of forgiveness
as it bubbles up near the brim of cups, and lids

As whispers shake free, falling from
Heaven's threshold
I place an intent ear to this heart
In hopes that one of those hushed messages is intended for me
Longing to hear it
Though often its vibration is too much to bear
Fate held within Earthy herbs & roots
Ancestral stars glimmer to message what is meant
Shimmers trickle down in an effort to heal us both
Past Lips.
Teeth.
Tongue.
With cascades of promises offered within each warm, trusting sip
With closed eyes and open hands Inhale deeply -
Penetrate Me.
Skin.
Lungs.
Breathing in sync, we are now balanced
Knowing we both can safely savor sweet solace here

Can I be your cup of tea?
Listening to the recollections with a sympathetic ear
Filling, and needing to be filled
With pains poured from these tired hearts
Love that ebbs and flows simultaneously
As we chance to drink in this fragile love
once more

Eulogy

Here lies my...
Star-crossed lover?
Long lost love?
Love of my life?
or *The One?*

I really don't know what to call you,
How to address you
These terms don't seem at all fitting now because they imply
a reciprocity -
A You & a Me
An Us, A We

I believed it then
Intensely, with my ever faithful heart
That's the part that still pains me
The fact that I fell
I allowed the fall to happen -
Swift
Hard
Blindly
Trying to forgive myself
For believing false sincerity

I should never be wanting to see you again
Banish all semblances from history
Hope to never cross paths inadvertently
Bury you deeply within the recesses
But it's quite the opposite

With every flashback
Every daydream
Every reverie
I long for the serendipity once more

Tragic, no?

Trying to convince myself that it's not you that I miss
But, instead, what I thought you represented
What I thought you were meant to be in this life

Caught in the seeming realness of happily ever after -
Horse and carriage, immaculately placed crown
Batted lashes with flirtatious flights of fancy
Rose-colored glasses focusing our gaze
Whirlwinds of butterflies & giggles
Deep breaths under starlit nights
Taking you in

False safety in warm embraces
And floods of kisses
Morph into this disappearance
An abrupt exit
Blindsided & backhanded
This tragedy -
A death of the truth?
Or the truth revealed in the death of us?
The death of who you presented,
Death of who you claimed you wanted to be

Tears cascade down pale cheeks
Flowing incessantly
Collecting like dew on these mourning petals
Rooted in grief, frustration and regret
Slowly penetrating this now contaminated soil

As all things living,
We have the ability to replenish
Bear fruit again
Feel love again
To fight off the diseased heart living beneath this breast -
Hard to hold onto when love's been torn away
She's very cracked
Repair is necessary,
And quite lengthy
For every piece that seems puzzled back into place,
There's many others still scattered without -
Waiting to be peace(d) back

Several others shattered to such shards
That I fear they'll never fit to become whole again
But, maybe that's the point -
Cracks are tangible evidence of lessons learned & loves lost

So what is to be mourned?
Your loss, or that of
My trust
My faith
My hope

If I will it strongly enough, can I ever get these back?
Am I being naive?
Very

Tragic, no?

Thusly, once again, here lies
My Star-crossed lover
My Long lost love
The Love of my life
The One -
My Heart,
May she find peace in her next reincarnation
Fragile as she is,
Those shards & splinters still reflect glimmers of Love & Light
Can't kill its hope even if we tried

There's beauty in her chiseled, mosaic'd fragments
She'll never be whole, seamless
But, she'll always be flooded in crimson
Rebirthed in Love
Manifested from within
Circulated throughout
Crafted to endure

Encanto

Lluvias de verano desde el interior de una caja de mosaico
Cubo Rubik en color y complejidad
Intenta mantener la calma a medida que la vulnerabilidad se filtra
Puestas de sol de melocotón y rayos de luz de luna
El sol logrando verme entre la oscuridad
Las hojas de árbol con volantes bailan en la brisa de la isla Como
los dobladillos de faldas alrededor de muslos
bronceados y tonificados
Las olas del mar coquetean con las costas
Acariciando la arena para recordarle de su belleza
Cada gránulo otra razón para darle las gracias al Señor
Troncos de árboles de doble hélice con ADN
Conserva los orígenes de nuestras historias
Susurrando cuentos de salud, dinero y amor
Los temas de las conversaciones nocturnas que solo los coquis
pueden compartir
entre la corteza, ramas y enredaderas
Transportando el sabor de la cultura en sus sistemas subterráneos
Arraigado en lo que parece ser la eternidad
Orgullo borinqueno
Bautizada en azúcar, agua de coco, chocolate y café fino
Empiezo a bailar bajo la lluvia en mis chancletas
Dándole las gracias a mis ancestros que me ahogan
con sus bendiciones de las nubes
Que me aplauden con cada paso que cojo, sin importar si voy
en pasos lentos
Sin destino en particular
Solo bebo de la agua bendita cayendo del cielo mientras continúo
viajando en mi camino...

Supongo que esto es lo que se siente cuando te dan la bienvenida
a casa.

Encanto (Charm)

Summer rains from inside a mosaic'd box
Rubix cubed in color and complexity
Tryin' to hold in the cool as vulnerability seeps out
Peach sunsets and moonlight spotlights
Sunshine managing to play peek-a-boo even in the dark
Ruffled tree leaves dance in island breeze
Like the hems of skirts around bronzed, toned thighs
Ocean waves flirt with shorelines
Caressing the sand to remind her of her beauty
With each grain being another reason to give thanks to the spirits
DNA'd double-helixed tree trunks
Hold the origins of our histories
Whispering tales of life, love and prosperity
The subjects of evening conversations that only the coquis can share
amongst the bark, branches and vines
That transport the cultural flavas in their underground systems
Rooted in what seems like eternity
Boricua pride
Baptized in sugar, coconut water, chocolate and rich coffee
I begin dance in the rain in my chancletas
Thanking my ancestors who drown me with their blessings
from the clouds,
Hearing their applause with every step I take, no matter
how slow my steps may be
No particular destination
Just drinking in the holy water sprinkles that fall from the sky
as I continue to journey on...

I guess this is what it is supposed to feel like when you're welcomed
back home.

Sola Una Gota

Nacida de una gota
Será de lluvia
De sudor
O de lágrimas
Pero estaba destinada a nacer

¿Cómo puede algo tan aparentemente simple contener tanta
posibilidad y afecto?

Creciendo las flores
refrescando su rostro
Dándole un éxito a la emoción
Aclarando la vista para realizar
Que todo se limpiará con el tiempo
Siempre podemos empezar de nuevo

Como las flores, las hierbas, las hojas
Que se van a dormir durante tiempos fríos, en tiempos difíciles
Para volver a despertar aún más hermosas,
Llenas de aún más vida
Con la llegada de su hermana, Sol, y su calor amoroso
Desarrolladas por dentro con la química y fortaleza de las gotas -
ya sean de lluvia, de sudor o de lágrimas -
que llevan por dentro de su núcleo

Hay quienes no me ven
Posiblemente nunca le importe querer
Ver la potencial que hay dentro de mi ser
Pero sé que hay una magia por dentro
La misma química que revive la naturaleza cada primavera
Y aunque aveces tengo que esconderme en tiempos difíciles
Aunque aveces parezco frágil y sin de permanencia
A pesar de que aveces siento que mi alma ha sido conquistada por
la negatividad que trabaja tan duro para rodearla

Sé que nací de una sola gota -
Ya sea de lluvia
De sudor
O de lágrimas
Pero, estaba destinada a nacer...

Y todo lo que se necesita es una gota consistente para desmenuzarse
la más dura de las piedras

Only a Droplet

Born from a droplet -
Be it of rainwater
Of Sweat
Or of tears,
But I was destined to be here.

How can something so seemingly simple hold so much possibility
and affection?

Blooming flowers
Cooling off your brow
Granting an exit for emotion
Bringing clarity to obscured vision
Helping one realize that everything will be cleansed in time -
We can always start again.

Like the flowers, grass and leaves
That slumber in frigid climates, in difficult times
To reawaken even more beautiful,
Filled with even more life
With the arrival of their sister, Sun, and her loving heat
Matured from within by the droplets -
be they of rainwater, of sweat or of tears -
They hold within their core

Jessica Diaz

There are those that don't see me
Possibly may never care to want to,
To see the potential that is within my being
But I know there is a magic inside
The same chemistry that revives nature every Spring
And even though I sometimes I have to hide myself in difficult times
Even though I sometimes appear fragile and lacking permanence
Even though I sometimes feel like my soul has been conquered by
the negativity that works so hard to surround it

I know that I am born from a single drop -
Be it of rainwater
Of sweat
Or of tears,
But I was meant to be here…

And all it takes is one consistent droplet
to chisel away
at the hardest of stones

Grounding

Under the black sky
Encircled by the night's stars
Peacefully, I sway
Within these truths is where
I stay

ACKNOWLEDGEMENTS

This journey has been long; but it definitely has not been traversed alone. "Thank you" is a phrase that cannot encompass the true level of gratitude and love that I have for all the people that have supported me - both in life & with this book. I cannot express how much it means to have you all in my corner - rooting for me, celebrating with me, making me feel seen & heard and comforting me when life is less than peachy. You have my heart always.

Shout-Outs, in no particular order, to:
Starting with My Framilia - *Friends who are Family.* Life is so much funner with you guys in it...

My ABC's! My brothas from anutha mutha: Aaron - little brother, Brock - big brother & Corey - twin brother. You gentlemen are truly the best brothers a girl could have wished for! It's hard to pinpoint when we officially became siblings, lol; but I'm ever so grateful that it happened.

Aaron, always so wise. You've helped me connect the dots in so many ways. I feel our bond has strengthened even more in the last 4 years or so; and I'm glad that it has. I admire your stoic resilience married with your teddy bear heart. Thank you for sharing all your sides with me.

Brock, fellow Aquarian! IYKYK! We be going IN on anything and everything, lol. You're always like, *"Damn, how do we still got things to talk about!?!"* That, I think, is the beauty of our bond. The fact that we have evolved together in so many ways - from our days as co-teachers to coaches and, now, as educational leaders, we're able to reflect on the past, see the now and have deafening hope for the future *(even when others try to convince us not to)*. We are always whipping up a plan, strategizing the next level *of the next level.* Thank you for always keeping it real, for helping to keep my vision clear and helping me grow as both an educator and a poet.

Corey, my road dawg adventure seeker. My fellow brunch enthusiast. My concert companion. The list goes on & on & on! I'm so glad you didn't give up on cracking my shell and making me your friend, lol. No matter what curveballs life has thrown my way, you are always the first person to help shake me back into my center, to remind me of who the fuck I am and that this will not break me. Thank you for your confidence, your acceptance and your endless encouragement. You'll always be My Sunshine.

Gentlemen, your pep talks, empathetic ears, thoughtfulness, brilliance and creativity keep me hopeful, grounded and secure. I know my parents are grateful that I have you guys here in this space to look out for their little girl. Thanks for having your hermana's back!

My Sisturrrs - Christine, Tanika, Marisol, Joyce, Elizabeth, Vanezza & Lissette
You ladies are my circle of sisters! In a world that can be so catty and competitive, pitting women against each other, I feel so blessed to have your friendship - to exist in this circle of nurturing love and admiration that we've created for each other.

Christine, we don't see each other often. But, I always feel how proud you are when I share my writing with you. I love how you always remind me of how proud my mom would be if she were still here to be experiencing all this on this Earthly plane. After almost 40 years of friendship (damn, lol), it is clear that our heart tie is a lifelong one that no amount of distance can diminish. Always remember that I'm cheering for you too!

Tanika, it was in your living room that I first got word that 2 of my poems were being published for the first time. While I sat there in shock, you were screaming, jumping up and down saying, *"You're a writer! I told you, you're a writer!"* Talk about being felt & seen! At a time where I was very apprehensive of taking on the identity of poet because: *How dare I be that bold? How dare I claim that publicly and possibly be terrible at it?* You were always there to remind me of my creative side - that it is present, and beautiful, and valid, and deserving to be shared. Another OG of my sister clan, you're a real one. One of the smartest and toughest chicks I know. Keep standing in your power, Gurl. Do you!

Marisol, Joyce, Elizabeth & Vanezza - Each of you a saucy, sassy spitfire in your own right, you all have inspired me in your life journeys. So multifaceted. So forward thinking. Breaking boundaries and paving new pathways for young women in each of your fields. I met each of you at different times in my life and, in that journey, there have been times where we haven't been as present or as close due to physical distance or life's circumstances. But, please know that I value your energy and appreciate your support. I will always consider you family, and will always be a part of your cheering section. Thank you for your essence. Such an honor to call you my sisters.

The OG Lil Sistur aka Cuzzo aka Ms. Stay Fly 24/7 - *Lissette*, I love your crazy ass! Thank you for always being a warm, nostalgic refuge for me. Every time we're together, I can't help but feel like we're 7 years old again. You keep me grounded in youthful whimsy, helping me hold onto my sillies. No matter how tough life can get, time with you and the kids always recenters me in what is most important - enjoying life, holding onto your happies at all cost. Thank you for sharing your infectious spiritedness with me.

Keith, my kindred spirit. Senryū gymnast, lol. The language of poetry connected us then, and it still does now. We've experienced a lot of life together in 6 years time. Thank you for the moments shared that granted me the peace & vulnerability to compose some of the poems within this collection. Your fingerprints are definitely on several of them. As modest as you are, I hope you realize how dazzling your spirit is. I am so happy that you're picking up your pen again. I can't wait to hear what you cook up! And, remember: Whenever, wherever, whatever - I got chu.

To My Creative Community - The Changemakers & The Visionaries: *Josue Caceres & BX Writers* - I've told you personally and shouted you out before. But, you really have no idea how much it meant and what it did for my spirit for you to have included my poetry in the first **BX Writers Anthology**. At that time, I was in a very funky place, searching for direction. My poems being felt and seen and shared really brought a part of me back to life. Thank You! #yerrrrrrrr

Davina Ferreira & ALEGRIA Publishing - The BEST IG follow everrrrr! Our crossing paths was such a lovely surprise! At the mid-way point of the pandemic, where I was working from home and trying to hold onto myself as well as continue to grow myself, the Universe placed your call for new writers in my feed. Since then, I have been consistently writing and reading and intentionally connecting myself to poetry, prioritizing that part of my life as crucial to my being. Thank you for supporting the creation of this book, helping to bring this Bronx girl's dream to reality.

DreamYard - To the entire crew! The magic you help cultivate across classrooms in our Bronx schools is unparalleled! Almost 20 years of Arts & Social Justice collaboration - be it in the classroom working with students, at the leadership level working with teachers or personally supporting each other in our individual creative endeavors, I've always walked away from our shared experiences feeling refreshed, proud and hope-FULL. You are my people! I will always be a loyal co-conspirator in your mission. Count on that!

An extra special hug to:
David Ciminello - My Mr. C! Bronx Writes Poetry Slam Champions forever! 2015 will always hold a special place in time. Our collaboration helped me find my poetry self again. The magic our kids birthed that year still brings happy tears to my eyes. I will forever be grateful for you. XOXO
Renee Watson - Your writerly journey is my inspiration! Your work - a revelation! Thank you for your inspiration, guidance and support to all of us blooming writers.
Ellen Hagan - friend & mentor, I love you! In all of the collaborations & celebrations we've participated in - both inside and outside of the classroom, you have always been equal parts gracious and glorious. I am truly thankful for your spirit. Thank you for always seeing me,

remembering me, reaching out, helping me connect to and immerse myself in creativity. Being in your orbit is always a joyous, safe space. Here's to many more years of connecting & creating!

To My Familia
Tio Papino - Your daily texts and check-in voicemails are cherished. Thank you for looking out for me in your way. Thank you for understanding and accepting that I do things differently, and still having my back anyways. I appreciate your support more than you know. You're the closest tie I have left to mommy so every hug, every heart-to-heart, every *"I love you"* and every *"I'm proud of you"* hits a little different. I love you, Tio.

Big brother, William - There's several layers to unpack. I don't think we're anywhere near scratching the surface. But, I appreciate your effort to reconnect, stay connected and start anew, in the now. I'm all in if you are. Thank you for supporting my poetry and for cheering on my pursuits. Here's to new beginnings…

And, finally, to my angels - my parents, Luis Manuel Diaz & Iris Diaz. *(Also lovingly known as Louie & Cuca.)* Everything I have done and continue to do is a result of you, and in honor of you. Every compliment or accolade I receive, I always attribute to the two of you. The smarts, the sarcasm, the humor, the groundedness, the loyalty, the work ethic, the joy and spiritedness - I got all that and then some from having you as my parents. I never planned to have to experience this much of my life without you physically being here. It's been hard. Really hard. But, I feel your love and guidance encircling me all the time - through memories, through dreams and through the subtle signs I know you're both responsible for me seeing. Please continue to hold me up and hold me down from your spiritual plane. I hope this collection makes you proud. I miss you - even the quirks that used to annoy me back then, lol. I love you. Te prometo que continuaré viviendo esta vida mía *con mucho salud, dinero y amor.* ¡Siempre!

ABOUT THE AUTHOR

Jessica Diaz - Educator. Advocate. Poet.

Latinx Artivist and Bronx-native, Jessica Diaz, credits her urban roots
and Puerto Rican heritage most for fueling her lifelong commitment
to education, advocacy and The Arts. Using poetry and storytelling
to raise awareness and empower the Self and the Culture, Jessica
strives to make a positive impact in whichever pursuits she is
immersed in, feeling it is her purpose to nurture and mentor young
people. Having had a love for writing since she was a child, Diaz's
energies turned specifically towards poetry in 2015 through her work
with her 5th Graders preparing for a poetry slam. In that experience,
the teacher became the student as she began to explore the same
poetic devices her students were engaging with in an effort to be in
the creative process with them. Here is where she realized that poetry
was a passion that had been in hibernation far too long and now
was the time to wake it up! With the spoken & written word being
her preferred Social Justice tools of choice, Jessica teamed up with

ALEGRIA Publishing to create her first collection, *ÓYEME*. This collection shares the lessons she's learned from her elders, spiritual guides and the raw realities of love & loss. Diaz believes that within these reflections is where the discovery of all the diverse, delicate and delicious intricacies that shape her identity are rooted. Throughout her creative processes, Diaz believes she has gained a deeper understanding of the criticality of introspection and hopes that in engaging with her poetry, readers will be encouraged to do the same. Some of Jessica's works can be found in the *BX Writers Anthology: Volume One & Two, Year Gone Hazy: Send-Offs to 2020, Asteri(x) Journal, The Sims Library of Poetry and Barrio Panther: Vol. 4*. Diaz has also performed at The Kentucky Women's Writing Conference: Wild Women of Poetry Showcase, Speak to Exist's Sip & Listen Poetry Slam, LTX Quest Conference as well as been a featured poet at Yuca Arts Presents: Time 2 Shine, DreamYard's Open Mic Series, Bronxlandia and, most recently, the spoken word play, *Latin América*, at The Hudson Theatres in Los Angeles through ALEGRIA Publishing. Jessica finds balance between work and play as an avid concert goer, "Sunday Funday" brunch enthusiast and world traveler on her time off. But finds as much peace & joy snuggling with her pug, Chauncey, and binge-watching documentaries and horror movies. Jessica still lives and works in The Bronx, committed to touching the hood first by supporting others in her community in finding their voice, their passions and discovering purpose.

Contact:
jessicadiaz2910@gmail.com

IG @jboogie193 - TikTok @j.boogie193